Stephen Franklin

A Time of Heroes 1940/1950

Canada's Illustrated Heritage

Canada's Illustrated Heritage

Publisher: Jack McClelland
Editorial Consultant: Pierre Berton
Historical Consultant: Michael Bliss
Editor-in-Chief: Toivo Kiil
Associate Editors: Michael Clugston
Clare McKeon
Harold Quinn
Jean Stinson
Assistant Editor: Marta Howard
Design: William Hindle
Lynn Campbell
Neil Cochrane
Cover Artist: Alan Daniel
Picture Research: Lembi Buchanan
Michel Doyon
Betty Gibson
Christine Jensen
Margot Sainsbury

ISBN: 0-9196-4426-0

N.S.L. Natural Science of Canada Limited
254 Bartley Drive
Toronto, Ontario M4A 1G1

Printed and bound in Canada

Let's Go . . . Canada! was the message on posters, and throughout the country people responded. Thousands queued up at army, navy and air force enlistment offices, if not always willingly, then because it was expected. Others took jobs in war industries, canvassed for Victory Bond campaigns, worked as farmhands out west or labourers in food processing plants, or knitted socks.

Contents

PROLOGUE	*Kilroy Was Here!*	6
ONE	*Homemade Banners*	10
TWO	*Maple Leaf Up*	24
THREE	*Wings*	36
FOUR	*The Newfie-to-Derry Run*	48
FIVE	*Canada Carries On*	56
SIX	*The Secret War*	68
SEVEN	*The Repats Return*	80
EIGHT	*Displaced Persons*	92
NINE	*The Atomic Age Begins*	100
TEN	*Canada's New Look*	112
	Acknowledgements	124
	Index	125
	Picture Credits	128

Who knows whether this Vancouver father and son ever saw each other again? Of those who went overseas, over 42,000 never returned to their families.

Threats of air raids black out B.C. coastal cities three nights.

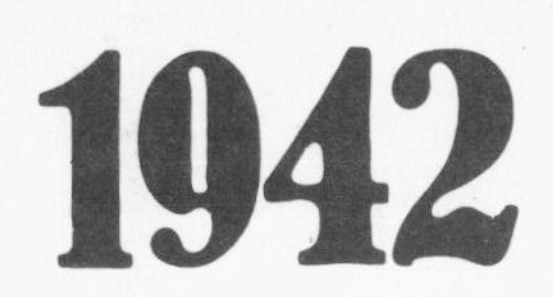

All persons of Japanese origin on the West Coast relocated to interior camps.

Food rationing begins with coffee, sugar, tea, meat and butter.

Shipshaw Power Plant on Quebec's Saguenay River begins operation.

Dominion plebiscite releases PM King from "no conscription" promise.

Canada's first synthetic rubber plant opens at Sarnia, Ont.

Bruce Hutchison publishes *The Unknown Canada*.

Canada goes on year-round Daylight Saving Time.

Canadian Art magazine publishes its first issue.

Alcan Highway from Dawson Creek to Fairbanks, Alaska completed after nine months of work.

JUNE 15 42

THIS IS NO PICNIC

WORKING AND LIVING CONDITIONS ON THIS JOB ARE AS DIFFICULT AS THOSE ENCOUNTERED ON ANY CONSTRUCTION JOB EVER DONE IN THE UNITED STATES OR FOREIGN TERRITORY. MEN HIRED FOR THIS JOB WILL BE REQUIRED TO WORK AND LIVE UNDER THE MOST EXTREME CONDITIONS IMAGINABLE. TEMPERATURE WILL RANGE FROM 90° ABOVE ZERO TO 70° BELOW ZERO. MEN WILL HAVE TO FIGHT SWAMPS RIVERS, ICE AND COLD. MOSQUITOS, FLIES, AND GNATS WILL NOT ONLY BE ANNOYING BUT WILL CAUSE BODILY HARM.
IF YOU ARE NOT PREPARED TO WORK UNDER THESE AND SIMILAR CONDITIONS
DO NOT APPLY
Bechtel Price - Callahan

Over 5,000 Canadian troops take part in ill-fated invasion of Dieppe: 900 dead, 2,000 captured.

Japanese sub shells Estevan Point on Vancouver Island; no damage.

Canada presents Britain with $1 billion in free materials, munitions and food.

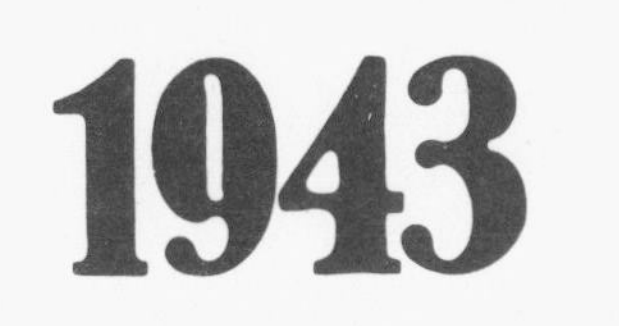

Johnny Longden of Taber, Alta. sweeps thoroughbred racing's Triple Crown aboard Count Fleet.

Canada plays host at Quebec Conference between Roosevelt and Churchill.

Zoot-suit toughs tangle with soldiers in Montreal.

Canadian Army Show makes its debut at Toronto's Victory Theatre.

Massive DDT spraying begins to combat spruce budworm epidemic in northern Ontario.

Canadian industry reaches nearly full employment as a result of war contracts.

Canadian 1st Division joins in Allied invasion of Sicily and begins the push north.

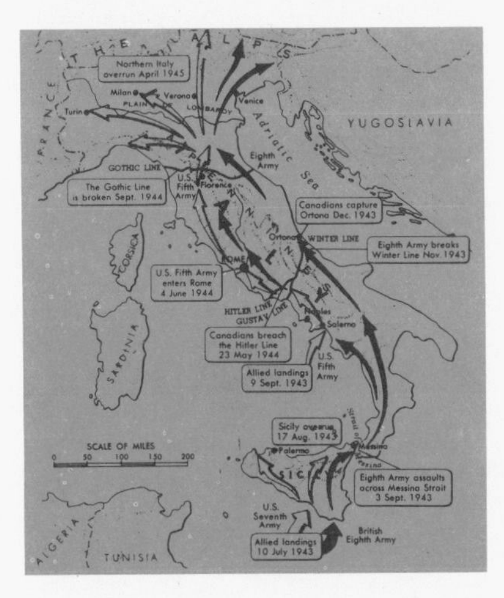

Canadian Mint issues 12-sided "tombac" nickels with the motto: "We win when we work willingly" — in Morse code.

Canadian mining magnate Harry Oakes murdered in the Bahamas.

Trans-Canada Airlines begins trans-Atlantic service.

1944

Tommy Douglas leads the CCF to victory in Saskatchewan.

THE LEADER-POST

DECISIVE C.C.F. VICTORY

SUPER BOMBERS SMASH AT TOKYO

41 to 4

Returns by seats

Regina sweep

Liberals swamped in tidal wave vote

Party standings

ALLIES SMASH NAZIS BACK

Mazo de la Roche publishes *The Building of Jalna*.

Department of National Health reports 300,000 cases of syphilis.

Nearly 30,000 Canadian troops take part in the invasion of Normandy on D-Day.

FOR CANADIAN TROOPS

THE MAPLE LEAF

OUR TROOPS IN HARD FIGHTING

Reds Advance take Narva fight for Lwow

HERE WE GO AGAIN!

Enemy Counters To Regain Ground

NORMANDY

Beyond St. Lo

Camp X established near Oshawa, Ont. as training base for Allied secret agents and saboteurs.

PM King introduces conscription for overseas active service sparking protest and riots in B.C. and Quebec.

General H. D. G. Crerar appointed Commander-in-chief of 1st Army.

Canadian Army begins liberation of Holland

A Time of Heroes

Son of the Group of Seven painter, Lawren Phillips Harris painted Tank Advance *while serving in Italy — one of 72 works in this magic-realistic style.*

Previous page: *Many of their fathers and brothers in the cockpits and turrets of real planes, thousands of boys assembled models like these printed in Winnipeg.*

Kilroy Was Here!

Private Turvey reporting, and would the gentlemen kindly remember he's just a Body, and so are all the other joes . . . And he's sorry about some of their language but the real guys talked a lot worse.

Earle Birney, *Turvey* (1949)

The so-called roaring twenties started in 1919 when the boys came home from the Great War. The hungry thirties were heralded by the stock market crash of 1929. And the forties, in their turn, began four months early, as Canadians looked forward to the Labor Day weekend.

At dawn on Friday, September 1, 1939, German troops and armour rolled swiftly into Poland, employing a new strategy of lightning-fast warfare soon known all too well by its German name, *blitzkrieg*. For three years Britain and France had watched while Germany re-occupied the Rhineland and took over Austria and Czechoslovakia. Finally, on September 3, the two powers declared war on Germany.

The Dominion of Canada did not automatically follow suit. In part it was an assertion of independence, and in part due to the difficulty of recalling Parliament for a special emergency session. Western MPS took advantage of Trans-Canada Air Lines' recently inaugurated trans-continental service, which flew seventeen passengers at one time. No highway stretched across Canada, so most of the others took the train.

Torchy Anderson of the Vancouver *Province* recorded the decision to go to war:

It was on Saturday night, September 9, during a casual, undramatic moment when the commons clock pointed to 10:23 P.M. that the country actually made its decision to enter its second world war . . . . This half minute of destiny, men may someday find the most important in the history of this young country. It passed without demonstration. Canada shouldered arms in silence.

When the division bells rang, one solitary figure – frail and white-bearded – voted against Canada's declaration of war. It was J.S. Woodsworth of Winnipeg, Methodist minister, social worker, founder and still leader of the socialist CCF party, and a life-long pacifist. He had recently watched as American and Canadian youngsters played together under the Peace Arch at the border of British Columbia and the state of Washington. He said simply: "I vote with the children."

His colleague Colin Cameron, MP for Nanaimo-The Islands, doubted that the 600,000 disillusioned unemployed would relish the war. "They will not join up," Cameron asserted. "Why should they fight for their own destitution?" It was a good question, but Tommy Douglas, MP for Weyburn, Saskatchewan, already knew the answer. Some

The rodent exterminator who issued this trade card didn't mince words in his hatred for Hitler. At fairs and carnivals the Führer's *face was a common target on the midway.*

The interior of this Trans-Canada Airlines Lockheed hardly has enough headroom for this stewardess to stand. During the war almost all passengers were military or government.

volunteers, he knew, enlisted for the new boots, greatcoat, two warm uniforms, three square meals a day and a private's basic pay of $1.30 a day, rising to $1.50 after three months. That was, after all, a seven hundred per cent increase over twenty cents a day on relief. Others left farms and homes and jobs because they believed that democracy was worth defending against totalitarian and godless regimes. Douglas had watched the boys "come out of the boxcars and go straight into the recruiting stations."

There were few marching bands, few flags waving, few loud hurrahs to see them off to war. Too many men remembered Vimy Ridge and the senseless slaughter incurred for a few acres of French or Belgian mud. In Ottawa the government thought in terms of "limited participation" – perhaps 40,000 troops, and a chance to sell more apples, cheese and bushels of wheat to Britain. The invincible army of France and Royal Navy (Britannia still ruled the waves) probably wouldn't need much more help.

In the end no one ever found a catchy adjective to attach to the forties, as they had for the two previous decades – and no wonder. It was the bloodiest and most destructive decade in the history of civilization. No Vandal, Goth or Tartar hordes had ever visited such desolation. Fifty million humans died, and for the first time in the history of warfare, more than two-thirds of them were non-combatants: nursing infants, children and young mothers; old men sunning themselves in the square; farmers, their wives and daughters; young men.

Overseas forty-two thousand Canadian men and women, most of them in their twenties, were killed in action or died of other causes. This was considerably fewer than in the previous war, yet a mere four per cent death rate was no consolation to those left behind. One Remembrance Day after the war, Mrs. John Boldus flew to Ottawa from

Vibank, Saskatchewan, to lay a wreath at the National War Memorial in Confederation Square. She represented all the Silver Cross mothers and war widows of Canada. On her coat she wore three Silver Crosses, one for each son lost with RCAF aircrews over France, Italy and Germany within a single year: Peter, a bomber-navigator; Martin, a flight engineer; and Johnnie, a gunner.

World War II was a time of tragedy and unique individual sorrow; of long separations and loneliness; of unbelievable barbarity; of fear, agony, boredom and longing.

It was also a time of heroes: a time of remarkable courage, endurance and self-sacrifice, when strong bonds were formed between men and fierce loyalties engendered – a time for the re-affirmation of the human spirit.

It was a time of small follies and momentous blunders, when a quizzical figure with a long nose and bald head peered over walls announcing "Kilroy was Here!" The most popular acronym was SNAFU (Situation Normal, All Fouled Up). It was a time of escape from uneventful lives lived in dull surroundings. It was a time when emotions were heightened.

The forties picked Canadians up from their accustomed hearths and tossed them about like fall leaves in the winds of war, separating husbands and wives, young lovers, fathers and sons, mothers and daughters – sometimes forever. For many of the country's 11,300,000 inhabitants, the forties was the most eventful decade of their lives. In that time Canada was transformed into a major industrial nation and became an active participant in international affairs and the world community. It was said that Canadians spent the first half of the forties making war and the second half making babies. The birth rate was the highest of any developed western nation, and the 2,700,000 increase in population was due almost entirely to natural increase.

In 1940 Stephen Leacock worked in the dawn hours above his boathouse on Lake Couchiching, finishing the final draft of his latest book, *The British Empire, Its Structure, Its Unity, Its Strength.* Meanwhile editors, advertising copywriters and luncheon speakers at Kinsmen and Kiwanis Club meetings depicted the Empire as a bandaged but defiant John Bull. By 1949 the bulk of the British Empire had been dismantled.

King George VI, a shy monarch, and his Scottish wife, Queen Elizabeth, reigned throughout the decade and were represented in Canada by the last three British governors general.

A Liberal government remained in power in Ottawa during the decade, and the Dominion government assumed vast new powers at the expense of the provinces. Ottawa unilaterally took over income and corporation taxes and succession duties and, by agreement, much of the responsibility for relief and welfare. The Dominion government introduced unemployment insurance and the Family Allowance Act.

In Saskatchewan the first socialist government in North America came to power under Premier Tommy Douglas in 1944, and the CCF moved into the official opposition benches in Ontario in 1943. As their memberships increased, labour unions began to flex their muscles. The Gross National Product rose twenty-five per cent between 1945 and 1948, and a new wave of immigration provided the necessary bodies for an expanding work force.

The exigencies of war and its aftermath brought about a major shift in emphasis in the Canadian way of life, away from Britain and toward the United States. This shift showed itself in new trade patterns, new defence agreements and even in school textbooks. There was no abrupt cutting of one pair of apron strings, and no conscious tying on of another pair. The shift was gradual and cautious, but it was there all the same.

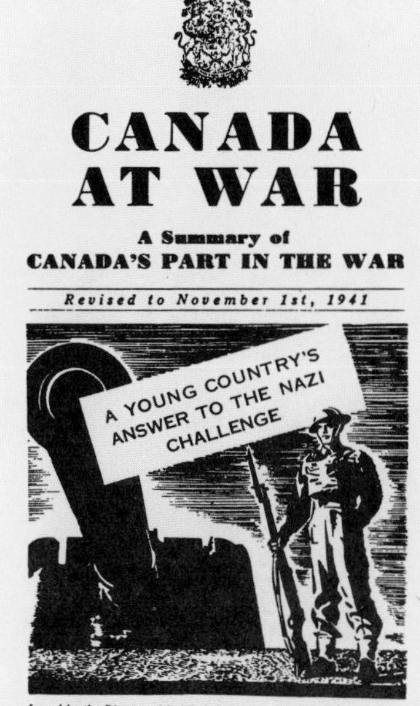

Canada at War *was the official clarion of the national effort, issued by the Wartime Information Board. Chock full of photos, facts and figures, and laced with morale-boosting copy, it was the slickest piece of propaganda printed and distributed during the war years.*

CHAPTER ONE

Homemade Banners

Night shift at the plant. The women
wear their hair pulled back in nets
and welders' goggles hide their eyes.

Joyce Nelson, "Home Front, 1942"

From Whitehall to Ottawa in the crisis summer of 1940 came an urgent message from Lord Beaverbrook, the dynamic Canadian-born newspaper baron who was Winston Churchill's new minister of aircraft production: "One aircraft today is worth ten in six months time."

In six months time, Beaverbrook feared, there might not *be* an England unless the Royal Air Force, outnumbered by the German *Luftwaffe*, had more fighter planes. Denmark, Norway, Holland, Belgium and France — all had fallen to the German invaders with terrible swiftness in ten weeks between April and June. Fascist Italy had entered the war on Germany's side, and Britain now stood alone in Europe.

Five thousand miles from the battle, at the Canada Car plant in Fort William, Ontario, the tempo of work accelerated dramatically. On the production line were rows of Hawker Hurricane fighters for the RAF. Bill Zeleny, who was in the tool and jig department, recalled: "We worked a seven-day week and overtime every night except on weekends. We clocked in at 8:00 in the morning and quit at 7:45 at night. But we only worked eight hours on Saturday and Sunday and we called them 'half-days'!" The old boxcar plant had been closed and empty for sixteen years. Now Nels Scaravelli, the timekeeper, was adding more and more names each day to the payroll: two hundred in 1938, six hundred at the end of 1939, six thousand by 1941.

Sixty per cent of the workers at Canada Car were women, and wolf whistles greeted every good-looking male who walked through the plant. Many were girls of nineteen or twenty, from small towns in Manitoba and Saskatchewan, who had been earning five dollars a month plus board keeping house back home. The Lakehead lured them with high wages, the excitement of war work and the chance to "do their bit." So many of them came it was hard to find accommodation, and five hundred girls lived next to the plant in Winston Hall, a big H-shaped dormitory built by Wartime Housing Limited, an Ottawa crown corporation.

The women worked as turret lathe operators, punch press operators, drillers, grinders and welders. They did the same work as the men and often did it better, Bill Zeleny admitted. "We had one girl crane operator on the ten-ton travelling crane and her touch was terrific. As for the teams of girl riveters on fuselage assembly, they could put the men to shame." Across town at the Port Arthur Shipbuilding Company, women swarmed over fourteen corvettes ordered by the Royal Canadian

Poster puns and celebrity-studded Victory Bond rallies sold the need to match patriotism with hard cash. Hollywood's reigning movie queen, Montreal-born Norma Shearer, and dozens of other stars attracted hundreds to fund-raising affairs.

Opposite page: *Single women were the first to be asked to "do their bit" by taking jobs in armaments factories. Ronnie Foster, voted Bren Gun Girl of the Year in '41, is making gun barrels at the John Inglis appliance plant in Toronto.*

Shortages in almost all resources and materials curtailed normal factory production, and most advertising reflected the change. During years of rationing and tight money, companies kept their names in the buyer's mind, advertising for a "some day" appliance-filled future.

Navy. They filled and capped shells in an old starch plant and worked out in the woods for Great Lakes Paper.

Canada Car turned out 1,650 Hurricanes, some of which were flown by Canadian fighter pilots in the Battle of Britain. By working without pay on two successive Sundays, the workers were able to donate two additional Hurricanes. It was their special contribution to what was called "the National Effort," an all-out campaign on the home front to hasten victory for the Empire and democracy.

Rosie the Riveter

Even the boss at Canada Car was a woman, although that was unusual. Brilliant, self-effacing Elsie MacGill of Vancouver was the chief aeronautical engineer, and under her supervision skis and wing de-icers were first fitted to a modern fighter plane. Later she introduced a desert version of the Hurricane, fitted with filters on the air scoop to keep out the sand.

Much later, after Pearl Harbor, American illustrator Norman Rockwell immortalized the women war plant workers on the cover of the May 1943 edition of the *Saturday Evening Post*. He portrayed a redhead with rosebud lips, a pert upturned nose and forearms mightier than wrestler Whipper Billy Watson's. She cradled a huge rivet gun in her arms, and across her lunch pail was painted the name Rosie. Rosie the Riveter became the symbol for all of them, American and Canadian, whether they handled a rivet gun or not.

War brought a kind of good times to Canada. In March 1940 there were still 612,000 Canadians on relief, and unemployment stood at almost ten per cent of the labour force. By 1941 there was work for all who wanted it. The twin cities of Fort William and Port Arthur both flourished. They were lunch-pail towns, where the payrolls were heavy with Ukrainian, Italian, French-Canadian and Finnish names, with fewer numbers of Poles, Hungarians, Scandinavians and Germans. On the production line at Canada Car the hourly rate rose from twenty-five cents in 1939 to fifty cents in 1940. That was big money; with overtime it amounted to forty or forty-five dollars a week. Women were paid the same rate as men. The United Auto Workers union made sure of that.

Some spent every cent they earned, even though every worker was expected to buy one five-dollar War Savings Certificate for four dollars every week. When the night shift came off at 1:30 A.M., some of the workers would head out to the nightclubs on the edge of town – Nash's or the Granview – or over to Kakabeka Falls and dance until five in the morning. There were dances three nights a week at the Elks Hall – mostly foxtrots, with some spot dances, "excuse me" dances and jitterbugging. The major shortage, as usual, was single men. At Christmas time, with the round of banquets and dances, turkey draws and parties, the girls would advertise in the Fort William *Times* or the Port Arthur *Chronicle*: "Escort wanted for dinner dance Saturday, all expenses paid."

a record harvest

In 1940, after years of dust and drought on the prairies, there was a record harvest. More than a half-billion bushels of wheat poured into the elevators at the Lakehead and out again by grain carrier across the Great Lakes. The port was busier than it had ever been and so were the CPR and the CNR. The railway was still the king of transportation. Long-haul trucking had not yet developed, and Trans-Canada Airlines' new transcontinental service was almost entirely reserved for official civilian or military travellers. Freight trains rumbled and clattered all night along the shore of Lake Superior, carrying the provisions of war to the ports in the East. Overcrowded passenger trains travelled in both directions, carrying troops on leave, troops bound for new bases, units heading overseas and wives and children joining their home-based husbands and fathers. There were line-ups in the dining cars and berths were at a premium.

The activity at the Lakehead was typical of activity all over Canada. In the last year of peace, the country had spent only one per cent of its national income on defence, and relied on Britain to supply its warships, warplanes and weaponry. By 1944 Canada had become the world's fourth largest producer of all the manifold instruments of warfare. And before the decade was over, Canada had emerged as one of the major industrial and trading nations in the world.

four thousand planes a year

Nowhere was this transformation more evident than in the Canadian aircraft industry, which turned from the manufacture of bush planes to the production of military aircraft. By 1943 the industry was turning out four thousand planes a year. The government's Victory Aircraft plant at Malton, Ontario, had a work force of ten thousand who built one big four-engine Lancaster bomber a day for the RCAF. When the Mosquito, the lightweight wonder-plane made of wood, went into production in 1942, it affected the fortunes of rising New Brunswick industrialist K.C. Irving. He had recently taken over a bankrupt company called Canada Veneers in Saint John, and the little company quickly became the world's largest supplier of hardwood aircraft veneers.

The growth in shipbuilding was equally dramatic. At the outbreak of war not a single ship was under construction in the country's sixteen shipyards. Canada's merchant fleet consisted of twenty-seven freighters plus eleven Imperial Oil tankers, and the country had never built fighting ships larger than minesweepers. In 1940 construc-

While the Allied and Axis armies were engaged in a deadly game of tic-tac-toe in Europe, the ad men used the game-fad to sell bonds.

Judging by the reactions in letters to editors of newspapers and magazines, it took some time for many to accept women in men's jobs. By 1942 women streetcar operators were common.

tion began on a fleet of corvettes and quickly progressed to frigates, escort ships and finally to sophisticated destroyers. At Montreal, Lauzon, Sorel and Quebec City along the St. Lawrence, at Collingwood, Kingston, Toronto and Port Arthur on the Great Lakes, at Esquimalt, Victoria and North Vancouver along the West Coast, eighty thousand men and women, working sometimes under floodlights, built 400 naval vessels and 393 big merchantmen to replace some of the thousands sunk by German U-boats.

the last McLaughlin-Buick

Of more immediate concern to the one in eleven Canadians who owned a car in early 1942 was the decision to halt all civilian car production and turn over the car plants to the production of war vehicles. Luxury cars had already been hit by an eighty per cent tax, and now the last of the splendid McLaughlin-Buicks rolled off the line in Oshawa, Ontario. World War II was highly mobile, and trucks, scout cars, Bren-gun carriers, armoured cars, universal carriers and three-ton artillery tractors were the essential wheels of warfare. Canada produced eight hundred thousand army vehicles. Every second vehicle used in the desert by the British 8th Army was made in Canada. Staff officers at Rommel's *Afrika Korps* headquarters issued special instructions to capture Canadian reconnaissance Jeeps since they did not get stuck in the sand as did the German ones.

The variety, complexity and sophistication of the armaments and materials that Canada produced amazed Britain and the Allies. They had expected steel from Hamilton and Sault Ste. Marie, nickel from Sudbury, and copper and zinc from Flin Flon. They had expected lumber, foodstuffs and raw materials. These they got. In 1942 Canada delivered ninety million bushels of wheat and over four million barrels of flour, as well as five million hundredweight of bacon and ham and seven million pounds of dried eggs, canned salmon, canned meat and cheese. The Alcan aluminum smelter at Arvida, Quebec, provided forty per cent of all the aluminum used by the Allies and was so vital that it was surrounded by anti-aircraft batteries.

What the Allies didn't expect, however, were naval guns, radar equipment, optical gunsights and torpedo engines – items Canada had never before produced. Donald Hings of Burnaby, B.C., patented a pioneer walkie-talkie set for tanks; Group Captain William Franks developed the world's first pressurized flying suit; Winnipeger Charles Goodeve, working with the Royal Navy, strung coils of copper wire around the hulls of steel ships, thereby saving them from German magnetic mines. At the University of Toronto, Arnold Pitt and R.W. McKay developed a miniature power pack for the proximity fuse. Until then it had taken an average of twenty thousand rounds of ammunition to shoot down one enemy aircraft. With the proximity fuse it took only four hundred "ack-ack" shells.

"dollar-a-year men"

After the Japanese army occupied most of the world's rubber plantations, Canada's Polymer Corporation built a $50 million synthetic rubber plant at Sarnia, Ontario. After the fall of France in June 1940, the Dominion government created a vast arsenal of war and trained tens of thousands of unskilled men and women in industrial techniques. Over a million workers – one tenth of the population – provided the sweat, and Ottawa provided the direction and control. This small, sedate city expanded dramatically, and the wartime government acquired enormous powers. In the first month of the new decade, Mackenzie King, the veteran Liberal prime minister, seized on criticism of his war effort from Ontario, and at the opening session of Parliament, he asked for dissolution and called a general election. The Liberal party won a clear majority and remained in power, unchallenged except from within, throughout the forties.

On the home front Canadians were affected most keenly by three blunt, pugnacious and indefatigable politicians. As minister of munitions and supply, C.D. Howe, an American-born engineer and businessman, created a great war machine. He was helped by expert industrial and business leaders brought in as "dollar-a-year men." Finance minister Jim Ilsley, a lean red-haired Nova Scotia Baptist, taxed the citizens of Canada to pay for the war. And Donald Gordon, at age thirty-nine a brilliant great bear of a man, applied the squeeze after October 1941 as chairman of the Wartime Prices and Trade Board.

fuzzy legislation

In early July 1940 hundreds of Canadians rushed to the altar to short-circuit another government squeeze – a piece of legislation that Mackenzie King had drafted one morning, presented to Parliament that afternoon and passed into law two days later. The National Resources Mobilization Act introduced military conscription for the defence of Canada (at home, not overseas) and conscription into war industry. The fuzzy legislation made it clear that married men would not be called, but it was unclear about what date one had to be married by. National registration for every Canadian man and woman over sixteen, except "cloistered nuns and mental defectives," took place in August. Within six months the army was calling up single men between the ages of twenty-one and twenty-four. The army turned down Winnipeg sign painter Bob Platt because of arthritis. The National Selective Service ordered him to Fort William, and four days later he was stencilling signs on Hurricane fuselages.

C. D. Howe
"Minister of Everything"

He was almost broke when he arrived in Halifax as a young professor of civil engineering at Dalhousie U., but by the time he was 40, he was a millionaire. He disliked politics, but by the time he retired in 1957, he had been minister of railways and canals, transport, munitions and supply, reconstruction, trade and commerce, defence production — "minister of everything," as many opposition MPs called him. C. D. Howe was born in Massachusetts, a descendent of Joseph Howe's cousin. A graduate of M.I.T., he left his teaching post in 1913 and turned his attention to designing and building grain elevators at the Lakehead. Coaxed into politics in 1935, he took on the management of Canada's war industries in 1940, and was one of the chief architects of the Allied industrial effort.

The National Effort

The extent of Canada's war effort at home has been tallied in dollars spent, guns, ammunition and vehicles produced, men and women employed in war industries . . . and dozens of others sets of statistics. However, numbers and percentages cannot tell the stories of miners working in sub-freezing temperatures, rivetters working the graveyard shift, or construction workers building the Alcan Highway. These stories would take a million words and a million pictures.

This woman is assembling air speed indicators in a Winnipeg parts factory.

Men and women sit side by side at the inspection table at CCM *in Toronto.*

War work wasn't all sweat and tears, as this beauty contest of assembly-line workers shows. The outfits of these women were standard daytime fashion.

Coffee, tea and sugar were the first items to be rationed, as the sign in this Montreal shop shows. After almost ten years of depression, shortages were familiar to most Canadians.

The Dominion government received much of its income from sales and excise taxes, and these were increased on a wide range of goods from phonographs, radios, cameras, cigarettes and liquor, to cars, cosmetics and carbonic acid gas (which boosted the price of soda pop from a nickel to six cents). In 1941 a single taxpayer earning $1,000 a year paid $87.50 in income tax. A typical married man with two children, earning a healthy $5,000, saw his annual tax soar from $80 to $700. In addition the government levied a special national defence tax ranging from five to seven per cent. The government also imposed a tough excess profits tax on business to prevent profiteering.

ration coupons

By the autumn of 1941 money was tight, and the cost of living had risen seventeen per cent in two years. In that year Canada became the first democracy to introduce almost total control of the economy: the Wartime Prices and Trade Board froze prices, wages and rents, and cut out frills on consumer goods and reduced the number of styles and models available. In 1939 Tip Top Tailors had sold men's suits with a vest and two pairs of pants for seventeen dollars. Because wool was scarce, the board outlawed double-breasted suits, vests, cuffs, pleats and flaps on pockets. Women's fashions assumed an equally streamlined look, with padded shoulders, small hats, and tight knee-length skirts.

The following year ration coupons for sugar, tea, coffee, butter and meat appeared. Yet most housewives visiting a modern Loblaw groceteria found little or no hardship involved. Mindful of the starvation in Europe, they knew how fortunate they were. The butter ration never fell below six ounces a week per person, nor the meat ration below one and a half pounds of choice cuts or two and a half pounds of cheaper cuts.

Gasoline rationing, at its lowest (120 gallons a

Women in the armed forces? The idea was preposterous, at least to old-line military brass. However, facing a shortage in personnel in the summer of '41, the RCAF *and the army formed women's divisions. These* CWACS *(pronounced "Quacks") from Ontario, B.C. and Alberta were the first of 2,900 to go abroad.*

IF NOT DELIVERED IN 5 DAYS

RETURN TO OFFICE OF MAILING

The world's greatest users of the telephone, Canadians found this message on their phone bills in the '40s, rationing conversation.

year) put a small crimp in driving the family car. The sale of all civilian tires and inner tubes had been halted in January 1941 and anti-freeze was scarce. Few people took vacations, expecially distant vacations, in the forties. Liquor rationing forced many to search for temperate aunts or teetotalling acquaintances who might be persuaded to take out a ration book on the seeker's behalf. Gin drinkers fared well in Nova Scotia where the ration was one bottle of rye or rum or two bottles of gin or two cases of Moosehead ale per month. In Ontario the ration was at one point reduced to a twelve-ounce "mickey" of liquor.

Victory stockings

Space was also at a premium. Hotel rooms and upper berths on sleeping cars were hard to find. With rents frozen, landlords asked for "key money" or insisted on selling a few sticks of useless furniture before they would rent an apartment. Used car dealers circumvented the law to sell prized vehicles. In 1944 the government forbade Canadians to move to certain over-crowded cities, including Victoria, Vancouver, New Westminister, Hamilton, Toronto, Ottawa and Hull, without permission.

It was hard in 1944 to find the right shade of lipstick or any silk stockings at all. Marion Foskett, a young Toronto model, went a whole year without wearing stockings because silk was needed for parachutes. "Nylons," made from the new miracle fibre, were only available if you knew somebody who knew somebody. In their place Victory stockings made of unprepossessing lisle were promoted. Some women resorted to "stockings in a bottle," painting them on like instant suntan. The trick was painting imitation seams down the back of the leg.

War was a time for volunteers. Volunteers worked in service clubs and canteens, did kitchen duty, served food and acted as dance hostesses for the half million men in uniform across the country and for lonesome Norwegian or Australian airmen training in Canada. Junior League volunteers in Montreal packed parcels for prisoners of war. Others constantly knitted socks and sweaters for the boys overseas.

There was a Milk for Britain fund in Vancouver and a Books for the Boys drive in Toronto. Housewives saved bacon fat and bones to provide glycerine for explosives and surrendered aluminum pots and pans to manufacture more planes. Husbands raided attics and basements for scrap metal and piled the loot on vacant city lots. Communities competed fiercely in their salvage drives for rags and paper. Children saved string and foil from cigarette and candy packages. At the dry cleaners one wire hanger had to be returned for another. Each summer students headed for the country to help on farms owned by men who were overseas.

$12 billion in Victory Bonds

Everyone from war heroes to movie stars urged Canadians to buy War Bonds and Victory Bonds. Montreal-born MGM star Norma Shearer put in her time on the Victory Loan platforms. Canny Canadians, uncertain how long the war would last and fearful of another recession when it ended, bought $12 billion worth. The war cost Canada $18 billion, but bonds paid a whopping two-thirds of the cost. Late in 1941 Canada gave a gift of one billion dollars to Britain. This remarkably generous gesture represented $87 per man, woman and child in the nation.

From Bill Zeleny to Norma Shearer, from Canada Car to Canada Veneers, from walkie-talkies to pressurized flying suits, Canadian people and resources were mobilized on the home front in a National Effort that was simply prodigious.

Rationing

Just as the country was pulling out of the post-depression blues, and people were again starting to have a few extra dollars to spend, the lid fell back on the economy. Wage and price controls, shortages in materials and rationing made everything from refrigerators to Red Rose tea scarce.

In the worst year of rationing, drivers filled their gas tanks once a month.

RATION BOOK 1

CARNET DE RATIONNEMENT 1

CANADA

Serial Number / No de série MS 105847

DOMINION OF / DU CANADA

Name / Nom Elizabeth Relyea

Address / Adresse General delivery

Longueuil P.Q.

Age if under 16 .... Age, si au-dessous de 16 ans

ISSUED BY THE WARTIME PRICES AND TRADE BOARD

EMIS PAR LA COMMISSION DES PRIX ET DU COMMERCE EN TEMPS DE GUERRE

In 1942 over 11 million ration books rolled off the presses — one per person.

Complex number and colour codes governed how much could be bought.

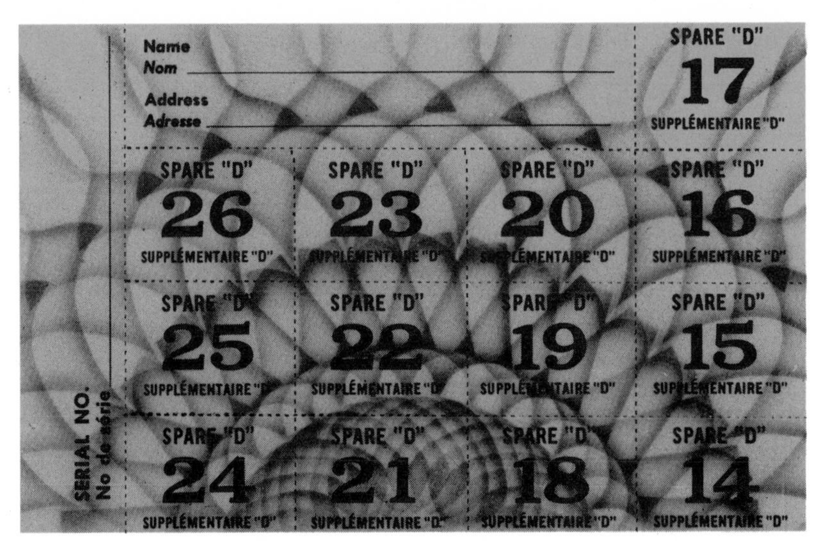

Despite the $5,000 penalty for misuse, the black market in coupons flourished.

At The Front

Military leaders who expected World War II to be much like the Great War were at first surprised to find little use for their former plans and tactics. The First World War had been fought from trench to trench by foot soldiers. Artillery was relatively short-range, horse-drawn caissons hauled supplies and ammunition, airplanes were somewhat of a novelty, wireless radio was haphazard, and the enemy's secret weapon was gas. In WW II everything was different: commando and guerilla tactics, V-2 rockets, 400-m.p.h. aircraft, super-bombers, submarines, radar . . . the atomic bomb.

"Red Patch" artillery-men load their field gun under camouflage netting in the autumn mud of Ortona.

D-Day, June 6, 1944: the 3rd Canadian Division, flanked by British and American forces, hits the beaches at Courseulles-sur-Mer, beginning the push inland.

CHAPTER TWO

Maple Leaf Up

. . . Canadians are going into battle again. When and where is one facet of the Great Secret.

Time Magazine, August 10, 1942

The vanguard of the 1st Canadian Division sailed from Halifax on Sunday, December 10, 1939, in a fast convoy of five ocean liners. No crowds lined the streets, no bands played, no flags waved. The departure was secret.

Few of the troops lining the guardrails of the Cunard liner *Aquitania* or Canadian Pacific's *Empress of Australia* had ever been overseas before. Many had never seen salt water; some had barely travelled more than a few miles from their hometowns. They wore the new battledress blouses that had so horrified the cutters at Tip Top Tailors two months earlier because of the sloppy, unmilitary cut. (Where were the tight-fitting tunics and brass buttons?) Their new "wedge" caps gave a right-sided tilt to heads recently savaged by army barbers. In their pockets were snapshots of families on porch steps, girl friends or wives.

The soldiers in this first contingent were nearly all native-born Canadians. Some were from the small peacetime army of 4,500 officers and men, but most were either Sunday soldiers from the 50,000-man militia or volunteers from the bread lines and relief camps of the unemployed. They disembarked in Scotland and travelled south through the tiny patchwork fields of the English countryside. They poked fun at the absurdly small trains, with their unfamiliar clickety-clack, smickety-smack rhythm, as they sped toward the same grimy army barracks at Aldershot where their fathers had lived twenty-five years before.

It was the coldest English winter in forty-six years – a damp bone-chilling cold. No matter. The men expected to be in Europe in a few weeks fighting Germans, even though the fighting was still sporadic. This was the "Phoney War."

In April and May the Germans unleashed their *blitzkrieg* on Denmark, Norway, Holland, Belgium and France, conquering each in swift and ruthless succession. Confusion reigned among the Allied forces. Canadian troops reached a Scottish port, en route to a counter-invasion of Norway which was called off. As the battered remnants of the British land forces were evacuated from Dunkirk, leaving behind their dead, their prisoners, their artillery, tanks and equipment, the 1st Canadian Brigade sailed for the peninsula of Brittany in a vain attempt to hold a bridgehead in Europe. They never met the advancing German army and returned to England two days later. France fell and Hitler now dominated western Europe. Mussolini chose this opportune moment to enter the war on Germany's side, adding further threats to the Mediterranean area, the Suez Canal and the life-

March music like the "Invasion March" was really a holdover from the Great War. The sound of the forties was big-band "swing" and soldiers' songs like "Mademoiselle from Armentières," "Lili Marlene" and "When the Lights Go On Again."

Opposite page: *Charles Comfort's painting* The Hitler Line *catches the vanguard of Canadian troops in May '44 breaking through enemy lines 50 miles southeast of Rome.*

lines of the beleaguered British Commonwealth and Empire.

It would be not a few weeks but three and a half years before this 1st Canadian Divison would see action, and then not in France, but in Sicily. And it would be four and a half years before the 3rd Canadian Division would land on the Normandy beaches on D-Day and begin the fierce battles of liberation northward through France, Belgium and Holland, along highways that bore the signs of the Canadian army: Maple Leaf Up.

In the late summer of 1940 the threat of German invasion loomed over England. There was only one division trained and equipped to meet the invaders – the 1st Canadian Division. Backing them up, short of equipment, was a Lowland Scots division plus the boys and middle-aged men of the Home Guard, who stood watch at night in fields of ripening oats, ready to fight German paratroops with shotguns and sporting rifles. In the aftermath of Dunkirk, shattered regiments were still re-forming, and the rest of the British army was scattered across a vast empire.

Vancouver cartoonist Cameron and other camp clowns had a field day with the mishaps in a private's private life. For a closer comic look, try Earle Birney's Turvey: *"Monday morning he was shaving by 0550 hrs, in water so cold he was surprised it could run. . . ."*

A-men and R-men

Back home in Canada the prospects seemed poor for Britain's survival. *Maclean's* magazine warned: "Canada could become the Belgium of the Americas. War might reach across the Atlantic step-stoning Iceland and Greenland." In Ottawa a worried Mackenzie King had introduced the National Resources Mobilization Act in June 1940. The prime minister assured his French-Canadian cabinet colleagues and the Quebec voters that he would not send the conscripts overseas. The following January the first group of single men aged twenty-one to twenty-four was conscripted into the army for the duration of the war.

There were now two categories of soldiers in Canada, the "A-men" and the "R-men." Active volunteers were training to defend Canadian territory. You could tell the difference at a glance. The volunteers sported the letters GS in a red circle on their sleeve. It stood for General Service, although the troops swore it meant "Gun Shy." The conscripts wore a maple leaf badge on their caps. The troops called them "Maple Leaf Wonders" or more derisively, "Mother's Boys." Nobody knows who first called them "Zombies," but gradually this became the common epithet hurled at them.

Knees Up Mother Brown

Often the A-men and the R-men trained together, slept in adjacent barracks, and pounded the same parade square. In the summer of 1941, the 19th Field Regiment, Royal Canadian Artillery, was mobilized, with batteries from Wingham, London and Guelph, Ontario. Full strength for a battery was 250 officers and men, but the regiment could only raise 150 volunteers. About 600 Zombies from Hamilton and Toronto reinforced the regiment at Camp Borden. Some of the conscripts volunteered to go active almost immediately. As training continued in Manitoba and British Columbia, the troops first encouraged and cajoled, then coerced and bullied the others into volunteering. All the dirty details went to the hold-outs. They built the camp at Terrace by day, stood guard by night and consistently pulled latrine duty. Of the 200 attached to the Wingham battery, all but eleven eventually sailed overseas with the regiment. Of course no one had forced them to go. They had "volunteered."

The build-up of Canadian troops in the south of England continued. By the end of 1941 there were 124,000 men. They sat around the barracks or went on interminable exercises and manoeuvres. They were billeted in modest homes where the bedsheets were as damp and cold as wrappers on a Mello-Roll ice cream, and in stately mansions where generations of aristocrats stared down at them from expansive portrait galleries. They sat in country pubs and acquired a taste for pints of mild-and-bitters beer served at room temperature. They learned to dance the Lambeth Walk, the Palais Glide and Knees Up Mother Brown, and taught eager young English girls to jitterbug. They chased girls, and the girls liked it, but inevitably there were brawls with British troops out on the streets of East Grinstead after the pubs closed.

The threat of German invasion had vanished by the end of 1940 and the war had moved to the Mediterranean. British troops fought in the desert of North Africa and tried unsuccessfully to stem the German invasion of Greece and then Crete. They fought the Italians in Ethiopia. They protected the oilfields in Suez, Palestine, Syria, Iraq and Aden. And where, meanwhile, were the Canadians? "Back 'ome in England, swipin' our girls, triflin' with our daughters, and foolin' around with our wives."

English girls took to the friendly Canadians. During the first year there were 1,222 marriages, and by the time the troops sailed for the Normandy beaches in 1944, 17,390 Canadians had married English girls.

pin-up photos

But the long wait also demoralized most of the troops. They wanted to fight; instead, they lay around the barracks sticking pin-up photos on the walls – Jane Russell, Ann Sheridan and Veronica Lake; Betty Grable, all legs in a white swim-suit; Rita Hayworth, red hair cascading over a black lace nightgown. Some overstayed their leaves going AWL; others deserted to the shadowy underworld. The famous Van Doos, Quebec's Royal 22nd Regiment, took over sentry duty outside Buckingham Palace. And still nobody saw action.

One reason was the Liberal government's de-

The first troops overseas were browned off by the long, inactive "sitzkrieg" in England, but they got used to it. Above, a soldier hams it up with his wife-to-be in a "swing wedding." Below, Canucks quaff a pint of bitter with locals. In Ralph Allen's Homemade Banners, *Pte. Mike Tully says he disliked the English for blackouts, Brussels sprouts, and for closing the bars at ten.*

Betty Grable, Rita Hayworth, Lana Turner, J. Fred Muggs (what's a monkey doing here?) and maybe even Alexis Smith. Alexis Smith? *Sure. She was the girl from Penticton, B.C., who starred in a dozen Hollywood films in the '40s, including* Dive Bomber *with Errol Flynn.*

sire to keep Canadian army units intact as a fighting force under Canadian command. The government bitterly regretted the first exception they had made to this policy. Ottawa had agreed to send two infantry battalions to reinforce the British garrison at Hong Kong. It chose the Royal Rifles from Quebec and the Winnipeg Grenadiers, reinforced with a hundred men from Saskatchewan regiments.

the "Gin Drinkers' Line"

The ill-starred contingent of 2,000 reached Hong Kong in November. On December 7, 1941, the day of Pearl Harbor, three battle-hardened Japanese divisions attacked. In seventeen days of savage fighting on the "Gin Drinkers' Line" and the slopes of Wong Nei Chong Gap, more than a quarter of the Canadian force died. Hong Kong was surrendered on Christmas day. Survivors were sent to Japanese prison camps. Those who survived the privations of the prison camps returned to Canada, emaciated shadows of their former selves. The Royal Rifles and the Winnipeg Grenadiers were the first Canadian army units to see action in World War II, and the only land forces to fight in the Pacific theatre of war.

The Japanese army then swept on to conquer most of the South Pacific islands and Southeast Asia in the early months of 1942. The Americans surrendered at Bataan, the British at Singapore, the Dutch in Indonesia and the French in Vietnam. Japanese bombs fell on Australia and Ceylon. India was threatened and most of China was in Japanese hands.

Elsewhere the outlook for the Alllies was equally bleak. In North Africa, Tobruk had fallen and 30,000 Commonwealth troops surrendered. Rommel's *Afrika Korps* was advancing toward Alexandria to conquer Egypt. The only effective military resistance in Europe came from Tito's partisans in the hills of Yugoslavia. On the eastern front Hitler's second offensive threatened Stalingrad and the vital Caucasian oilfields, without which Russia would have had to surrender.

This was the situation, black and complex, when the Dieppe raid was planned and executed. The August 19, 1942 raid on Dieppe, a seaport in northern France, consisted of a direct frontal assault carried out without previous bombardment from naval guns or bombers. One German war correspondent who witnessed the raid wrote: "As executed, the venture mocked all rules of military logic and strategy." He was not far wrong. For the 5,000 Canadians from seven regiments of the 2nd Division who formed the core of the 6,000-man assault forces, Dieppe was a massacre. Five years later, the *New York Times* paid tribute to the Canadians, describing Dieppe as a sacred spot "where brave men died without hope for the sake of proving that there is a wrong way to invade. They will have their share of glory when the right way is tried."

blazing, bloody battle of Dieppe

Canadian Press war correspondent Ross Munro, who rode in one of the landing craft, reported: "For eight raging hours under intense Nazi fire from dawn into a sweltering afternoon, I watched Canadian troops fight the blazing, bloody battle of Dieppe . . . . " What the censors would not let him write, had he wished to, was that he had seen the Royal Regiment of Canada wiped out on Blue Beach at Puys, mown down by murderous crossfire as they leapt from the landing craft. Only a handful were able to stagger up the pebble beach in the daylight to crouch below the sea wall. Half the 554 officers and men of the Royal Regiment died on the beach. Only twenty-two returned to England unscathed.

There were countless acts of endurance and bravery at Dieppe. Lieutenant Colonel Cecil Merritt led his men of the South Saskatchewan Regiment across an exposed bridge at Pourville, calm and bareheaded, swinging his tin hat at his side through the enemy fire. Rev. John Foote, padre of the Royal Hamilton Light Infantry, helped at least thirty wounded men to board evacuation craft, but stayed behind himself to be with the wounded and the prisoners. Both men received the Victoria Cross.

Freya

The casualty rate among the Canadians at Dieppe was seventy per cent. Of the 5,000 Canadian troops in the action, 3,400 were killed, wounded or captured. Yet Hitler subsequently tied up thirty-two German divisions along the coast because he feared Dieppe might be the prelude to a full-scale invasion.

Under cover of Dieppe, the Allies had carried out a vital secret mission. A new German radar system was causing heavy losses among Allied bomber crews. The system called *Freya* was different from anything the Allies had. As the Canadians assaulted Dieppe, a sergeant and nine men of the South Saskatchewan Regiment led a Jewish Cockney radar expert to a *Freya* station above Pourville. They had orders to kill him if he was in danger of capture. The operation was a success and with this new radar information, the Allies were able to devise counter-measures. One such tactic was known as "window," in which showers of silver foil were dropped from the bombers to fool the radar system. But it was small compensation. Dieppe was one of the tragic blunders of the war.

Canadian troops saw no action for eleven months after Dieppe and morale problems grew worse. A bitter joke going the rounds was that the 1st Division was the only outfit in military history

Andrew McNaughton
General "Andy"

His troops thought him Canada's answer to Patton and Montgomery, but he never led them into combat. As commander of the 1st Canadian Army, he was criticized for being too friendly with his men, for his "unmilitary bearing," and for his persistence in keeping the Canadian fighting units together — an issue over which he locked horns with the Allied high-brass and his defence minister, J. L. Ralston. Although he had proven himself a capable officer in WW I, and had directed the armed forces in peacetime, he was recalled in December 1943, and was forced to resign. Embittered by the action, he nevertheless agreed to replace Ralston when the defence minister resigned, and after the war served as head of the Atomic Energy Control Board and Canada's first United Nations delegate.

Dieppe...Ortona...Caen...Brussels

The list of place names reads like a summer holiday bus tour through Europe, but for three years thousands of Canadian troops sweated and froze in dozens of these cities and towns. Most of them would rather have been home in Trois Rivières or Moosomin. "It's a grim war, this," said Nova Scotia's Angus Macdonald. "It seems to lack the gay quality of the last one." For the frontline sons of fathers who had died on these same battlefields, the remark made little sense.

One of the war's costliest military blunders was the August 1942 invasion of Dieppe. Over 6,000 troops were thrown into action, 5,000 of them Canadians. As the invading armies were hitting the beaches, well-placed and prepared German batteries mowed them down. Over 900 Canadians died; 2,000 were captured.

Under fire on the road north to Ortona, Italy, the sergeant in this 4 x 4 looks for enemy emplacements. The roof-top turkey is for Christmas, they hope.

Minutes before the invasion of Normandy, some of these men try to hide tension by joking. Bicycles were intended for a quick dash from the beach inland.

No doubt about what this guard from the Régiment de la Chaudière *is thinking! D-Day and the victories of Normandy turned the tide against the Germans.*

In cities house-to-house fighting marked the Allied push through Europe. At left, the Canadian soldier is firing a captured German Schmeisser into a shelled house.

whose birthrate was higher than its deathrate.

The long wait ended in July 1943 when the Allies invaded Sicily. The 1st Canadian Division and 1st Tank Brigade landed at Pachino as part of General Montgomery's British 8th Army. There was little opposition during the landings, but in the mountainous interior the Canadians were matched against German Panzer grenadiers.

The village of Assoro clung to the side of one mountain, making it ideal for the Germans to defend. A frontal attack would have been suicidal and a thousand-foot cliff protected the German rear. An assault company of the "Hasty P's" – the Hastings and Prince Edward Regiment – was called on to scale the cliff at night in full gear without making a sound. The Hasty P's were victorious and dislodged the enemy. But it was a hard battle, a foretaste of the fierce fighting to come after the Canadians crossed to the Italian mainland in September and advanced northward.

Message urgent

du Commandement Suprême des Forces Expéditionnaires Alliées

AUX HABITANTS DE CETTE VILLE

Afin que l'ennemi commun soit vaincu, les Armées de l'Air Alliées vont attaquer tous les centres de transports ainsi que toutes les voies et moyens de communications vitaux pour l'ennemi.

Des ordres à cet effet ont été donnés.

Vous qui lisez ce tract, vous vous trouvez dans ou près d'un centre essentiel à l'ennemi pour le mouvement de ses troupes et de son matériel. L'objectif vital près duquel vous vous trouvez va être attaqué incessament.

Il faut sans délai vous éloigner, avec votre famille, pendant quelques jours, de la zone de danger où vous vous trouvez.

N'encombrez pas les routes. Dispersez-vous dans la campagne, autant que possible.

PARTEZ SUR LE CHAMP!

VOUS N'AVEZ PAS UNE MINUTE A PERDRE!

As ground forces fought from town to town, flyers overhead showered French cities with leaflets that warned of air raids. The intent was twofold: to prevent civilian loss of life, and to convince the enemy their defence was futile.

house-to-house fighting

Casa Berardi, an obscure hamlet on the road to Ortona, was the key to the whole 8th Army advance on Rome in December 1943. With eighty-one men from the Van Doos and seven tanks from the Ontario Regiment, Captain Paul Triquet of Cabano, Quebec, had orders to take and hold Casa Berardi. After several hours of fighting, Triquet rallied his surviving young French-Canadians and said "We are surrounded. The enemy is in front of us, behind us and on our flanks. The safest place for us is the objective." There were fourteen survivors when they took Casa Berardi, and only nine after they held it against repeated counter-attacks for two days. Triquet won the Victoria Cross, and the Allies moved on to Ortona.

The house-to-house fighting and the tank battles in the streets of Ortona halted briefly while the men ate Christmas dinner. Ortona was the bloodiest battle the Canadians had yet fought in Italy. There were other hard-won victories as the Allies continued their slow, inexorable advance northward. Each victory took its toll of front-line troops. Reinforcements arrived slowly. Wounded men returned to the line too soon. The men on the front lines cursed Ottawa politicians, army brass-hats and the Zombies who were safe at home.

D-Day

June 6, 1944, D-Day. A Canadian parachute battalion was the first to drop. Next, assault waves of 3rd Division and 2nd Armoured Brigade, the men still queasy from the choppy water, stormed ashore onto the Normandy beaches at Courseulles, St. Aubin and Bernières-sur-Mer and struck inland toward their objectives, Carpiquet airport and the city of Caen. The German armour was concentrated around Caen facing the Canadians and British. The next day the Germans counter-attacked. As the Canadians advanced through the Normandy wheatfields, they confronted the fanatical Hitler Youth troops of the 12th SS Division. In separate incidents that day, General Kurt Meyer's troops shot more than a hundred Canadian prisoners. From then on little quarter was given. Caen fell to the Canadians and British after thirty-three days of fighting. Advancing south, the Allies closed the Falaise Gap and encircled the German 7th Army. It was late in August. The battle for Normandy was finally over.

Normandy cost Canada 18,400 casualties, among them more than 5,000 dead. The casualties were higher than expected and the need for reinforcements from Canada grew more urgent. The 1st Canadian Army moved north, clearing the channel ports of France and Belgium. On the soggy polders of the Scheldt estuary surrounded by dikes, the Canadians fought for five weeks to open the great port of Antwerp to Allied shipping.

Then they swept on to liberate Holland.

With the infantry and the tank crews went all those other vital elements of a mobile modern army: the sappers and gunners, the signal corps, the intelligence officers and truck drivers, the loggers in the Canadian Forestry Corps, the Canadian Women's Army Corps, the medics, doctors and nurses.

Jean Ellis, a young war widow from Victoria, B.C., was one of the Red Cross workers who served alongside the nursing sisters in hospitals and at clearing stations throughout Europe. They served tea and cigarettes to the wounded. They wrote letters for them and occasionally read them "Dear John" replies from wives or sweethearts who had not waited. They struggled to treat SIWS (those with self-inflicted wounds) and those who had intentionally contracted venereal disease to escape action. They suffered through sudden attacks of the "Normandy Glide" or "Dieppe Dance" for which the unofficial cure was several swigs of Calvados.

crossing the Rhine

Meanwhile back in Ottawa late in 1944, pressure was mounting on the prime minister to send the conscripts to the battle lines. King fired his defence minister, Colonel J.L. Ralston, in a vain attempt to ward off the decision. But when a last desperate recruiting drive failed, the cabinet ordered 16,000 Zombies overseas. Many of the Zombies from Quebec and the Prairies deserted, holing up in barns, farmhouses, summer cottages or caves. In the dying months of the war, 9,500 reached Europe and of these 2,500 reached fighting units.

They were sorely needed, for by now the Canadians were crossing the Rhine, advancing into the very homeland of the man who had started this whole affair.

While other Allied forces were aimed toward Berlin and Munich, Canadian troops wallowed in the mud of Holland's polders. The North Sea supply route was critical to the armies, and to Canadians fell the thankless task of freeing the ports. Through November 1944 they fought dike to dike. In April '45, when their tanks rolled into Arnhem, Holland was freed.

Paul Goranson's sketch of this dorsal gunner on a Wellington bomber is one of nearly 200 pieces the Vancouver artist created while serving with the RCAF *from December, 1941.*

The Air War

"Just before dusk we assembled at headquarters for briefing. As the crews filed in through the door, everyone glanced at the map on the wall behind the dais, where the route for the raid was marked out in black tape. Moose would take the stand and call for silence while the roll was called; then the briefing began. First he would give us general facts about the raid; then the Intelligence officer would outline the nature of the target and the reasons for the attack, and finally Moose would run over tactics. He usually ended up by saying, 'Enemy fighters — I don't think you'll have any trouble with them. Good luck.'

"This time we were to bomb the docks at St. Nazaire, now a German submarine base. Takeoff would be at dusk. Dressing up was a long process for the gunners; it was a cold ride in the turrets and they wore as much clothing as they could. On top of this went a Mae West buoyancy jacket and parachute harness.

"It was getting dark. All around the perimeter navigation lights showed, and engines began to cough. The ground crew stood with thumbs up. One circuit of the field, and we set course climbing."

(Jerrold Morris, *Canadian Artists and Airmen*)

Not all of Canada's war art was "official" or painted on paper, panels or canvas. Quebec artist Albert Cloutier, stationed in Newfoundland and Labrador with the RCAF, *found this piece of fuselage art by a Lancaster crewman distracting competition for his own more serious work.* *(See also page 45.)*

CHAPTER THREE

Wings

If this is where I get mine, up there where it is cold and clear, on a battlefield where the dead don't lie about and rot, where there is no mud and no stench, where there is no moonlight by night, stars, and in the day . . . a blue sky above . . . if I get mine up there, there must be no regrets. I would have it that way.

Fuller Patterson

The most dashing and most dangerous of the three armed services was the Royal Canadian Air Force. It was manned entirely by volunteers and there were always more of them than the RCAF could accommodate. The attraction was easy enough to understand. For the past two decades, earthbound boys from coast to coast had followed the exploits of the famous bush pilots and watched barn-stormers perform their death-defying aerobatics over small farm fields. After all, no fewer than ten of the top twenty-one Commonwealth air aces in World War I had been Canadian.

Now, a generation later, Canada had her own small air force. In 1939 its permanent strength was 3,100 officers and men. Of its eight squadrons, only one reconnaissance squadron was fully trained and equipped for operations. Most of its 210 aircraft were obsolete: only thirty-six modern planes were fit for any sort of combat. Even under an accelerated program that year, the air force had managed to graduate only forty-five pilots.

This was the situation on December 17, 1939, when Prime Minister Mackenzie King announced that as its major contribution to the war effort, Canada had agreed to train 20,000 Commonwealth crew members a year in the increasingly specialized skills of fighter and bomber pilots, observers, navigators, bomb-aimers, wireless operators and air-gunners.

The British Commonwealth Air Training Plan was, in the words of the Montreal *Star*, "well nigh staggering." The plan required 40,000 qualified instructors, mechanics, armourers and other ground personnel; 3,500 trainer planes; and 210 schools and 97 air training bases, including runways, hangars and barracks on farmlands, open bush and stretches of bald prairie across the entire country. It cost the country a tenth of its national income, which then stood at only $3.5 billion annually. Within six months the urgency of the task increased as France fell and Britain was unable to send a promised 1,500 Anson training bombers across the Atlantic.

The plan was a remarkable success. In less than five years, 131,000 crew members won their wings. In Washington, D.C., on the third anniversary of the plan, President Franklin D. Roosevelt saluted Canada as the "Airdrome of Democracy." Forty-two thousand men of Britain's RAF came to Canada to learn to fly. Not all were Britons; among their ranks were young Poles, Belgians,

The RCAF came into its own in the war years, and with it the music of "To The Stars," based on the air force motto. Canada's WW I aces had flown with the RAF.

Opposite page: *Canadian pilots and navigators examine dots on a map, in William Dring's painting* Zero Hour. *Within the hour they will be thundering over the battle zone.*

The RCAF*'s No. 413 Squadron was transferred in April 1942 from Norway to patrol the Indian Ocean against Japanese attack. Here, A. L. Lumsden is at the guns of a Catalina flying boat.*

Czechs and Frenchmen who had somehow escaped their conquered lands.

For civilians living near the air bases, the thousands of young strangers streaming into Canada were a steady reminder of a distant war. Vancouver citizens dug deep into their pockets and bought fourteen trainer planes for the Elementary Flying Training School at Sea Island. Winnipeg hostess Mrs. Sally Cannell kept regular open house for overseas airmen from the base at Rivers, Manitoba; among her guests was a young Welsh airman named Richard Burton who would later go on the stage. Many of the RAF men immigrated to Canada after the war, among them Sergeant Arthur Hailey, who would write the television drama *Flight into Danger* and the best-selling novel *Airport*.

Aussies in "passion purple"

At "Little Norway" on Toronto's harbourfront, where a little girl named Liv Ullman played, there were 3,500 personnel from the Royal Norwegian Air Force. One year they received 800 invitations to Christmas dinner from Canadian families. Four thousand Americans crossed the border impatient to join in the programme, and more than 16,000 rangy New Zealanders and jaunty Australians in their "passion purple" uniforms trained in the country. For the thousands of Canadian girls who knew nothing but hometown boys, the plan was a bonanza of dates, dances, romances, and sometimes weddings.

It was even more exciting for Elaine Leiterman and the 17,000 other women who joined the women's division. She was eighteen when she left Timmins, Ontario, for the RCAF wireless school in Montreal, where she studied the innards of transmitters and receivers and became a radio telephony operator. At the large training base at Centralia, Ontario, where she was first posted, there were fine quarters, a kilted RCAF band and young Bermudians, Australians and South Africans in training. At her next posting in isolated Pennfield Ridge, New Brunswick, there was little but the Bay of Fundy, an abundance of fog and the cramped radio truck out on the airfield where she stood watch, talking to pilots aloft and giving them markings to fix their position. Sometimes there was a life-or-death urgency to her work. Once an aircraft from a nearby base was returning from a long sweep over the North Atlantic where it had been hunting U-boats. Fuel was low and the plane got lost, but Corporal Leiterman gave the pilot the homing directions and brought the aircraft in.

More than half the graduates from the Commonwealth Air Training Plan were Canadians, described by Air Minister Charles "Chubby" Power as "the very cream of the youth of Canada . . . . " One of them was Flight Lieutenant Dick Audet from Lethbridge, Alberta, who towed drogue targets and became a skilled Spitfire pilot.

deadly "Doodle Bugs"

On December 29, 1944, Audet spotted a formation of twelve Messerschmitt 109s and Focke-Wulf 190s flying in line astern. He shot down five and became an ace in ten minutes, a feat never duplicated in the RCAF or RAF. Nine weeks later, his score now at eleven hits, he drove his Spitfire at an enemy train and was hit by ground fire. Dick Audet was dead at twenty-two.

Edmonton's Wing Commander Russell Bannock was the RCAF's top night fighter pilot. In the summer of 1944, when the Germans launched their V-1 flying bombs against England, his squadron shot down eighty-two of the deadly "Doodle Bugs," most of them at sea where they could do no damage. In their Mosquito, Bannock and his navigator accounted for nineteen hits.

For the men in the RCAF Coastal Command,

Bomb aimers on a Halifax bomber were supposed to pick out enemy supply depots and artillery emplacements from this height after a glance at a map and a peek through the scope. Most hits were a mixture of luck and sighting, as the toll of civilian casualties sadly shows.

No1CNS

the sea was their battleground. They logged thousands of hours in endless sweeps over the water, searching, usually in vain, for U-boats, enemy surface ships, survivors in lifeboats or downed airmen aboard inflated dinghies. From the Aleutians to Iceland, and from the Gulf of St. Lawrence to the Indian Ocean, the twenty-seven squadrons of the Coastal Command sank a total of nineteen enemy submarines in six years of war.

"the Saviour of Ceylon"

One of the Command's more enviable exploits involved Flying Officer K.O. Moore, who hailed from Rockhaven, Saskatchewan. Two nights after D-Day, Moore was patrolling off the coast of France when a submarine contact was reported twelve miles ahead. He took his big bomber down to a hundred feet above the waves, straddled the surfaced *U-626* with depth charges and sank it. He had scarcely finished searching for survivors on the moonlit sea when he made a second radar contact. Once again he pressed home his low-level attack. It was as successful as the first. Just twenty-one minutes after the first contact, K.O. Moore had sunk two U-boats. No other aircraft or ship ever matched him.

The man they called "the Saviour of Ceylon" was also a Coastal Command pilot. Squadron Leader Leonard Birchall of St. Catharines, Ontario, was a career RCAF officer who had graduated from the Royal Military College in Kingston in 1937. In March 1943, No. 413 Squadron was transferring from the Shetland Islands to the British naval base at Ceylon. Birchall flew his Catalina on the long hazardous flight to Gibraltar, Cairo, Karachi and Colombo, rested a day and was sent on a patrol of the Indian Ocean. He was about to turn homeward when the moon rose, and he decided to make one last sweep to the south. He spotted dark specks on the horizon. As he flew closer those specks grew into the largest battle fleet Len Birchall had ever seen–Japanese battleships, aircraft carriers and innumerable cruisers and destroyers all steaming toward Ceylon 350 miles away.

The seasoned RCAF skipper had barely signalled their position on course, speed and size before Japanese Zeros shattered the wireless set and forced his crippled Catalina down onto the water. Beset by sharks and machine-gunned in their dinghy, Birchall and five of the crew survived. The Japanese pressed home their attack on Ceylon on Easter Sunday. Forewarned, the units in Ceylon drove them off. It was a major turning point in the war. Birchall received the DFC. He also survived interrogation and beatings in a Japanese prisoner of war camp and was awarded the OBE for his conduct as a prisoner.

The RCAF by now had forty-eight squadrons overseas. Spitfire pilots in the Digby Wing were flying fighter escort for American Maurauders on daylight raids. In sixty sorties over Europe they shot down forty-five *Luftwaffe* fighters without losing a single Spitfire. Other Canadian squadrons flew with 2nd Tactical Air Force in support of the PBI ("poor bloody infantry"). TAF pilots strafed enemy troops and tanks, dive bombed strong points, blew up bridges and gunned columns of transports on country roads, taking the heat off the fighting men of the 1st Canadian Army.

night raids

The largest and most lethal operational force of the RCAF was No. 6 Bomber Group, which carried out thousands of night raids on German cities. Of the 13,036 Canadian airmen killed in overseas combat, 9,980 were in Bomber Command. From quiet villages in the rolling Yorkshire countryside, the four-engine bombers took off at dusk, droning across the North Sea to devastate Hamburg and Bremen, destroy the great Krupp armament facto-

Typical of salvage campaigns in all cities, Winnipeg organized transit workers, school children, teachers and housewives, and earned almost $400,000 from recycling garbage. In Toronto a glue manufacturer did a brisk business removing "dead or worn-out horses and cattle promptly free," and selling glue to assembly plants manufacturing plywood planes.

Opposite page: No wives, mothers or domestics to do the laundry here, but this tin Nissen hut was home for many RCAF flyers. Among the amenities was something missed by many troops billeted in draughty British homes — "central heating."

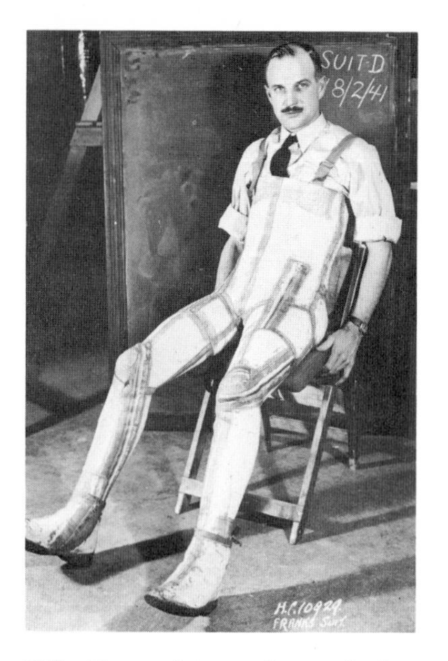

"Blacking out" in combat resulted in the loss of aircraft and pilots until Dr. Frederick Banting, the co-discoverer of insulin, and his team of researchers at the U of T devised a flying suit that could absorb changes of pressure at high speeds and altitudes. Above, Dr. W. R. Franks of the research team wears the water-filled G-suit.

The crew of a Lancaster bomber consisted of seven airmen: (left to right) a rear gunner, a wireless operator, a navigator, a pilot, a mid-upper gunner, a bomb aimer and a flight engineer. This is the crew of the "P for Peter."

ries at Essen and penetrate into the heart of Germany to bomb Munich or Berlin, Frankfurt or Düsseldorf. The cramped, unpressurized, lightly-armoured bombers were stripped for the maximum bomb load. They were buffetted by flak from anti-aircraft fire. Searchlights pinpointed them. German night fighters attacked them. They made their run and dropped their load. Some of them limped home with two engines missing, a navigator dead, sometimes on fire leaving a blazing trail across the inhospitable sea.

As the most northerly unit in RAF Bomber Command, No. 6 Bomber Group always had the farthest to go, the farthest to return. Among its heroes were two flight sergeants commissioned overseas. Both were Manitobans, blue collar workers of immigrant stock, and both were mid-upper air gunners. Peter Engbrecht was three when he and his parents arrived from Russia. He worked as a blacksmith until he joined the RCAF. From his turret over the fuselage of a Halifax bomber, Engbrecht became the only air gunner in the world to shoot down five enemy planes, a feat hitherto reserved for fighter pilots. For it he won the Conspicuous Gallantry Medal.

Polish-Canadian Andy Mynarski had been a leather worker in Winnipeg before he volunteered for aircrew at twenty-five. A week after D-Day his Lancaster was one of two hundred bombers sent on a low-level midnight raid on the French railyards at Cambrai. At 2,000 feet on the way in, the bomber was hit, two engines were knocked out and the mid-section of the fuselage caught fire. The skipper ordered the crew to bale out. As he was about to jump, Mynarski noticed tail-gunner Pat Brophy trapped in his turret and staggered back through the flames to free his friend. Drenched with blazing hydraulic fluid, he strug-

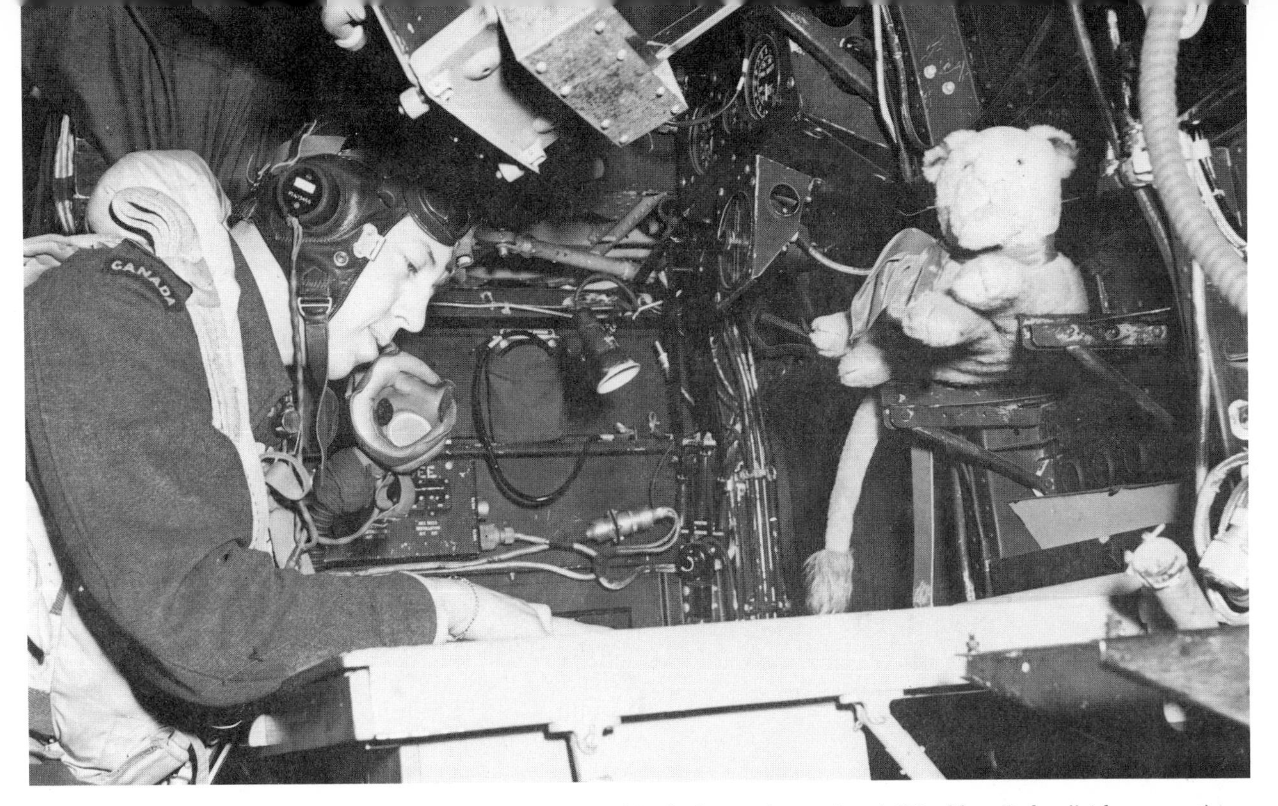

Navigator Gus Utas, like many other airmen, kept his good luck charm close at hand. "Ruthless Robert" (the mascot) wasn't much good at reading strange maps, but it often took more than skill to survive a bombing mission.

gled bare-handed with the jammed turret until he was driven back. At the escape hatch, he stood at attention and saluted Brophy. As he jumped, flames from his flying suit licked around his parachute. Mynarski died on the ground of burns and injuries. When the Lancaster with its full bomb load crashed into the trees, Brophy was miraculously thrown clear and survived. When he told his story, Andy Mynarski was awarded the Victoria Cross posthumously.

By all odds the greatest of the bomber pilots was Group Captain John Fauquier, who voluntarily demoted himself from Air Commodore to fly a third operational tour and won the Distinguished Service Order three times. In the late twenties, Johnnie Fauquier had given up the good life of a young Montreal bond salesman to establish his own bush flying outfit in the lusty northern Quebec mining town of Noranda. He flew with his friend John David Eaton, until Eaton had to go back and mind the family store. In 1942, when he led his bomber squadron in the first saturation raid on the city of Cologne, he was a seasoned thirty-two years of age.

An Australian flyer described Fauquier as "a press-on man, if ever there was one." Once when his squadron was suffering heavy flak in a raid on Bremen, he put his huge Lancaster into a power dive from 12,000 feet to ground-strafe the searchlight crews and anti-aircraft batteries like a fighter plane. He earned the title "King of the Pathfinders" in the great raid on the German rocket base at Peenemünde on the Baltic Sea, a raid in which some of the best German rocket scientists were killed and German plans to destroy London were set back by a full year. The work of the Pathfinder squadron was to indicate the targets to the incoming bombers by dropping flares. As

Buzz Beurling
"Screwball"

Other pilots called him "Screwball," the papers called him "Buzz" (it sounded better), and Canada called him hero. The only Canadian pilot at the top of the WW II "aces" list, George Frederick Beurling began flying at age 14 near his home in Verdun, P.Q. He soloed at 16, and before the war took aerobatics lessons from WW I ace Ernst Udet. It took Beurling until June 1942 to get into combat, and when he did, it was not with the RCAF (they had turned him down) but the RAF in Malta. The term "Screwball" fitted him to a tee: he was a maverick, a loner who hated military discipline. Instead of the gyro gunsight, he used his head to calculate his angle of fire, and shot down 33 enemy aircraft before he was grounded. When the war ended, he still itched for combat and left to join the Israeli Air Force. En route from Rome, his plane crashed and he was dead at 26.

The RCAF's *No. 401 Squadron of twelve Spitfires takes off from an airfield in England, en route to France. In October, 1944, this squadron combined to shoot down one of the* Luftwaffe's *new wonder-planes, the Messerschmitt 262 (the world's first jet), over Nijmegen, Holland.*

Pathfinder leader, Fauquier made no fewer than seventeen passes over the heavily-defended target area and remained there an incredible thirty-five minutes as the target for intense ground and air fire.

Fighter pilots were a different breed. The greatest Canadian fighter pilot of World War II was a man the RCAF rejected because he didn't have enough education, although he had beaten two top RCAF pilots in an Edmonton aerobatics competition only a few months earlier at the age of eighteen. A tall, lean Quebecker, his name was George "Buzz" Beurling. As a young boy Beurling had done odd jobs around the hangers at Cartierville airport to earn a buzz around the airfield with one of the pilots. He soloed at sixteen and a year later took a freight train to British Columbia to take aerobatic lessons from the great German ace, Ernst Udet. When the Finnish air force rejected him because he did not have his parents' permission to join, he worked his passage across the Atlantic as a deckhand to join the RAF. But he had forgotten to take his birth certificate, and he made two more Atlantic crossings to pick it up. The RAF accepted him, and posted him to the Island of Malta, where the life expectancy of a Spitfire pilot was very short.

a lonesome maverick

In the only siege in history conducted solely from the air, the Germans and the Italians had been battering Malta for two years. Almost starving, the pilots lived in caves or sat in the sweltering heat of their cockpits waiting for the next attack. Proud, confident and a lonesome maverick, Buzz Beurling scrambled into the sky over Malta during the long summer of 1942 and shot down twenty-eight enemy aircraft. He was a master of deflection shooting. His fighter was fitted with a gyroscopic gunsight, but fellow pilots said he never used it. He could work out angles of deflection faster in his head.

Hit twice in his last action – going to the rescue of another Spitfire – Beurling had to bale out and was rescued from the sea, amid a hail of bullets. He returned to Canada a hero, an officer despite his protests, his tunic adorned with the slim ribbons of the Distinguished Service Order, the Distinguished Flying Cross, the Distinguished Flying Medal and Bar. The reception was wild.

achievement of the RCAF

Eventually he persuaded the RCAF to let him make one last operational tour. He raised his score to thirty-one victories. Disciplined for making too low a pass over his own airfield, he resigned in May 1944. The RCAF was relieved. He was too unorthodox, too prickly, too much a loner, too dangerous an example for the young new pilots. After the war, Ottawa blocked Beurling's attempts to fly with the Nationalist Chinese Air Force against Mao Tse-tung's Communists. Finally in 1948, he made his way to Rome to fight for the fledgling Israeli air force. On take-off there, with three former *Luftwaffe* pilots aboard, his plane stalled. Buzz Beurling and his companions all died.

Canadian pilots with the RAF made a significant contribution to the age of heroes. The achievement of the RCAF was equally impressive. The force that had started out in 1939 with 3,100 personnel and a couple of hundred obsolete aircraft grew to become the fourth largest air force among the Allied powers. By mid-1944, RCAF strength numbered a quarter of a million, but the Canadian dream of an RCAF under independent command was never realized in the war years. No matter. The flyers were fighting the enemy the best way they knew how, and political views were of no consequence in the air.

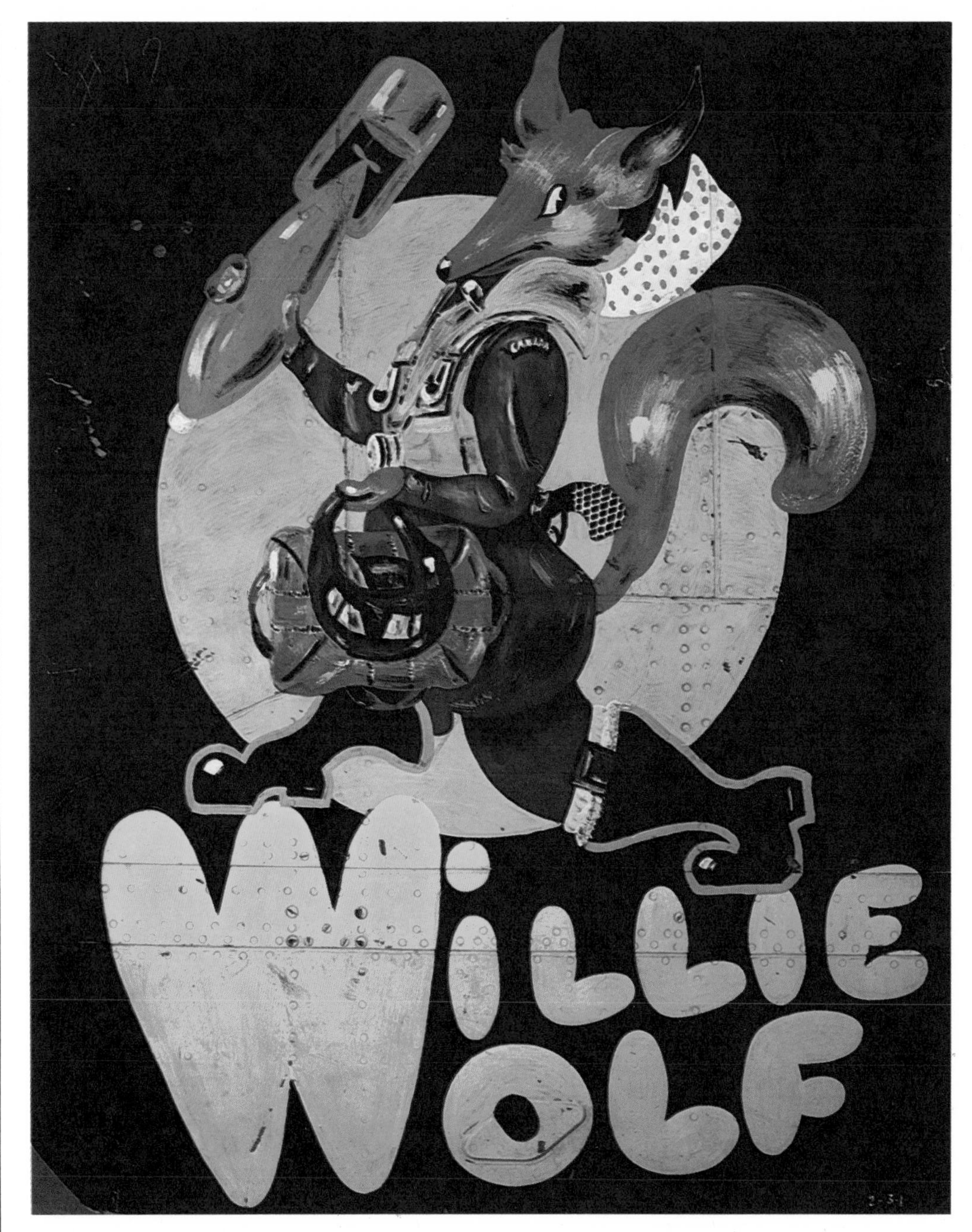

Besides the official markings and camouflage on aircraft, fighter pilots and bomber crews decorated the fuselage with personal insignia and unit markings. "Willie Wolf" and "Xotic Angel" (page 47) are among the few Canadian paintings to have survived the scrap heap.

The Battle of the Atlantic

"All day long the ship had been crashing into mountainous seas . . . Now she had a list to port and was taking in more water than the pumps could handle. You look over to where a tall column of orange-red flame shows a sinking tanker. You feel sorry for the guys in the tanker . . . maybe some'll get away . . . that'll make 'em better off, you think, than if they'd been in that ammunition ship that went up on the last convoy. . . ." William Pugsley, *Saints, Devils and Ordinary Seamen*

"Operation Overlord," the invasion of Normandy, used every class of naval vessel to transport men and artillery across the channel. The scene in Rhino Ferry *looks chaotic, but the operation was a well-planned success.*

In one of the most dramatic battles of the Atlantic, the Canadian destroyer HMCS Assiniboine *chased the German sub* U-210 *in and out of the fog for hours. For another hour they jockeyed for position, their deck guns blazing, but in the end the* Assiniboine *rammed the U-boat twice, sending it to the bottom.*

The seamen in Tom Wood's painting Guns Crew *look a little "green around the gills" after rolling around the Atlantic on convoy duty. Jokesters claimed that corvettes were so unsteady they would "roll on wet grass." Despite the reputation — and the often-seasick crews — they were the "sheepdogs" of the Atlantic.*

CHAPTER FOUR

The Newfie-to-Derry Run

Eternal Father, strong to save,
Whose arm doth bind the restless wave
Who bidd'st the mighty ocean deep
Its own appointed limits keep:
O hear us when we cry to Thee
For those in peril on the sea.

This hymn sent a shiver through even the most godless sailor whenever it was sung by ships' companies at parades from Halifax to Londonderry. It was sung with more than usual fervour in the dark months of 1942, when German U-boats attacked North Atlantic convoys with relentless success, and the Battle of the Atlantic hung precariously in the balance.

The Battle of the Atlantic lasted over two thousand days. It began on the first day of the war when a German submarine torpedoed the British liner, S.S. *Athenia* off the coast of Ireland, just twelve hours after the British had declared war. It ended almost six years later as Canadian warships escorted the German submarine *U-889*, flying a black flag of surrender, into harbour at Shelburne, Nova Scotia.

On this cold grey battleground, beset by summer fog and winter gales, Canada's sheepdog navy fought to protect the convoy system and keep open the lifeline of supply to Britain and Russia. If that lifeline were broken even for two or three weeks – if oil and gasoline, food and armaments, steel and synthetic rubber could not be carried across the Atlantic – Hitler would win the war.

Newfie-to-Derry, that was the most famous convoy run, and in 1941, U-boats torpedoed and sank a thousand merchantmen in the Atlantic, among them modern freighters, oil tankers, ammunition ships, ore carriers and rusty old tramp steamers. The following year they sank twice that many. The crisis stretched on into 1943, through a winter that was the stormiest in the North Atlantic for thirty years. There were still areas in the mid-Atlantic – the notorious "black pits" – that were too far from Newfoundland, Iceland or Britain to enjoy air cover. In September 1942 the veteran destroyer HMCS *Ottawa* was torpedoed twice in ten minutes and went down with 114 aboard. In October a single slow convoy sailing out of Sydney, Nova Scotia, at a speed of six knots lost fifteen ships in four days on the mid-Atlantic.

In December the destroyer *St. Laurent* and five Canadian corvettes were escorting a westbound convoy, already thinned down, through the black pits. A pack of U-boats attacked. The night sky was soon ablaze with flames from burning tankers and tracer shells criss-crossing the columns of ships. In the bitterly cold water, where five minutes' immersion was often fatal, merchant seamen bobbed in life rafts with small red beacon lights. In two hours nine Allied ships were sunk while the U-boats remained untouched. At dawn

Departure dates and times of ships anchored in Canadian ports were closely guarded secrets, and there is little evidence that loose talk led to any losses. However, from December '41 to May '43, U-boats sank over 5,000 merchant ships, many of them in coastal waters.

In heavy North Atlantic seas, especially in late autumn, even "old salts" had to hang on. Weeks later, in sub-zero weather, part of the job was chopping ice off the guns and rigging.

the senior officer signalled the surviving ships in convoy to try to escape independently if they so desired.

The convoy system was threatening to collapse. For every U-boat sent to the bottom, eight more were built and launched from German shipyards. But the Canadian navy, its ships pounded and buffeted by constant storms and badly in need of repair, its unseasoned crews near the limits of human endurance, grimly held on. That summer, as Allied power, technological superiority and experience mounted, the tide began to turn in the Battle of the Atlantic.

"meadow green lads"

When the war began the Royal Canadian Navy had a fleet of five coal-burning minesweepers and six British-built destroyers. Total manpower was barely enough to provide the ship's company for a single battleship. Backing them up were some 500 of the volunteer reserve, all enthusiastic amateurs, and less than 200 seasoned seafarers from the merchant service.

The key to this rapid expansion was an unlovely ship designed in England in 1915, put aside and revived in 1939, upon which Winston Churchill bestowed an ancient and honoured French name, the corvette. Designed for anti-submarine patrols in coastal waters, the corvette was never intended to cross an ocean. The corvette was uncomfortable and overcrowded, but it was simple and easy to build.

In 1940, as Halifax harbour lay crowded with British battleships and French cruisers, Polish destroyers and Dutch warships, Canada was building a fleet of doughty little corvettes. When Lieutenant Commander Alan Easton commissioned the corvette HMCS *Baddeck* at Quebec in 1941, only one of his three officers had ever been to sea before, and three-quarters of his ninety-seven-man crew had never so much as sniffed salty air. None of them had experienced the power of the ocean or felt that sense of eternity which the sea can bring to men on the watch before dawn.

"Meadow green lads" – that's what Lieutenant Commander Joseph Schull called them. After twelve weeks at HMCS *Cornwallis*, the big training ship at Digby, Nova Scotia, young landlubbers knew only the bare rudiments of working a ship and young stokers were not overly familiar with a ships' boiler room. They trained on the job, shepherding a convoy of fifty merchant ships out of Bedford Basin, northward to Greenland's Cape Farewell, then eastward toward Iceland and a meeting point with British escort ships.

Lying in their hammocks, they listened to the hammer blows of the sea against steel bows that sounded as thin as eggshells. Mess decks were littered with wet sea gear: sweaters, sea boots, socks, duffel coats and oilskins that never seemed to dry. Hot food from the galley aft was cold after it was carried forward across the open deck. Bread turned green with mold. Fruit, vegetables, even the meat rotted.

ice one foot thick

Many were too seasick to care. The watches – four hours on, four off, twenty-four hours a day, day after day – became a nightmare. A corvette, it was unfondly said, would roll on wet grass. In a North Atlantic storm, corvettes rolled, shuddered and wallowed on the terrifying sea. In the perpetual gloom of winter gales, the seas came green over the fo'c's'le and turned white in successive sheets on the gun turret, stanchions and lifelines until the ice was sometimes one foot thick. Seamen had to chip it away with pick-axes and hammers to keep the ship from keeling over.

The strain on the officers was even greater than on the sailors. Gales broke up the neat columns of the convoy, scattering darkened ships across the sea, increasing the risk of collision and decreasing the protection offered by navy escorts. During the summer off Newfoundland there was the terrifying prospect of colliding in the fog. That's how HMCS *Windflower* (named for the prairie crocus), the first corvette launched in Canada, was lost off the Grand Banks, struck amidships by a freighter. Moments before it sank, a boiler exploded, scalding to death many of the stokers down below in the engine room.

Sometimes at night torpedoes struck two ships so nearly simultaneously that it seemed to the rest of the escort force that only one had gone down. Such was the fate of the corvette *Spikenard* on the first Newfie-to-Derry run. It was five hours before the loss was discovered and by then nine-tenths of the crew had drowned or perished of exposure.

rich new killing ground

As more and more corvettes and leaner, twin-screw frigates joined the growing RCN fleet, they took their names from Canadian towns instead of flowers: *Arvida, Guelph, St. Boniface, Swift Current, Revelstoke*. Bonds grew between the town and the distant ship that carried its name. The town's mayor received a replica of the ship's crest; the townswomen knitted mitts and sweaters and seacaps, baked cakes and packed parcels for their sailors; volunteers collected books and magazines for them; girls wrote letters to and swapped snapshots with sailors they had never met. And if the ship sank, the entire town mourned the men who were lost.

For the people of the Gaspé and the Maritimes, the war at sea crept even closer. When the United States entered the war, Canadians were hopeful it would ease the burden on weary RCN escort ships. The reverse was true. While the United States had been neutral, U-boats had kept clear of

While escorting tankers north from Imperial Oil's Venezuelan ports, HMCS Oakville's *soundings picked up U-94, and depth charges brought the submarine to the surface. Too close to keep an angle of fire on the U-boat, the frustrated crew hurled Coke bottles at the enemy, then boarded with pistols and forced the Germans to surrender.*

According to the fine-print prices, you had to have $6.50 before you could afford to keep what you knew under your Stetson. Brocks and Kensingtons started at $6 and $5.

From a pre-war "strength" of thirteen ships manned by fewer than 2,000 sailors, the Canadian navy grew to a fleet of

North American coastal waters and the Caribbean, but in the months after Pearl Harbor, German submarines moved into this rich new killing ground. The American navy moved most of its Atlantic fleet to the Pacific to counter the threat from Japan, and freighters steaming northward from Baltimore, New York and Boston were left at the mercy of German U-boats. Canadian corvettes were diverted down through the West Indies to protect them, and new convoy runs opened up southward to Boston.

From Liverpool, Nova Scotia, to Miami, Florida, people along the coast could regularly watch the glow of torpedoed ships blazing at sea. In five months, U-boats sank 500 ships, 200 of them within sight of land. Survivors huddled together in lifeboats adrift off the Nova Scotia shore. Hastily-formed militia units stood guard against possible German landing parties.

In May 1942 the submarine *U-553* sailed into the Gulf of St. Lawrence as far as Anticosti Island and torpedoed the British steamer *Nicoya* and the Dutch freighter *Leto*. The Battle of the St. Lawrence had begun. Censors in Ottawa reported only one sinking. To admit more would give valuable information to Berlin. Yet Gaspé villagers of St. Yvon and Chloridorme had succoured more than seventy-five survivors with blankets and hot drinks, including a young woman and her baby who had miraculously drifted ashore alone in one of the *Nicoya's* lifeboats. In the absence of official statements, wild rumours began to circulate: U-boat crews were reported coming ashore regularly to dance the night away with French-Canadian girls; spies were skulking in every cove; a troopship was reported sunk with the loss of 6,000 Canadian soldiers.

In August skipper Paul Hartwig at the peri-

over 400 craft and 100,000 men. Hardly visible here, the frigate Swansea *chalked up many victories for the record.*

Artist Jack Chambers titled this drawing "Joining the Immortals" to commemorate the sinking of the St. Croix *— a tale of chilling coincidence. In September 1943 the ship was hit by three torpedos and went to the bottom. Her crew was picked up by the British corvette* Polyanthus, *which was also torpedoed. The 81 survivors from the* St. Croix *and one from the* Polyanthus *were taken aboard the frigate* Itchen, *but two nights later it too was hit. Only three men survived — one from each ship.*

scope of *U-517* launched a six-week reign of terror in the St. Lawrence. He sank an American army transport off the bleak shore of Labrador, and the Canadian freighter, *Donald Stewart*, enroute to Goose Bay with cement for the big airfield being built there. Hartwig sailed up the St. Lawrence to within 200 miles of Quebec and sank vessels off Rimouski, Matane and Métis. Other unidentified U-boats took part in the raid. The RCN steam yacht *Raccoon*, pressed into service as an escort, disappeared with all hands. In a swirling September mist, Hartwig torpedoed the *Charlottetown*, which went down in three minutes with half her crew. In Newfoundland, a U-boat sailed into Conception Bay and torpedoed two iron ore ships tied up at the docks of the Wabana iron mine, then repeated the raid a month later. Many U-boat navigators were ex-masters of ore ships who in peacetime had loaded iron at Wabana for the Krupp factories in Germany.

By far the worst disaster in the Gulf of St. Lawrence was the sinking of the Newfoundland ferry ship *Caribou*, outward bound from Sydney to Port-aux-Basques. One of the 137 casualties was Nursing Sister Agnes Wilkie, assistant matron of the naval hospital at St. John's, who was returning from leave in her Carman, Manitoba, hometown. Her friend, Margaret Brooke, kept Wilkie afloat in the freezing waters for two hours by clinging to a raft until her strength gave out. Brooke was awarded the MBE for her heroic efforts. Although some 2,500 Canadian nurses served close behind the battle lines in Italy and Northwest Europe, Agnes Wilkie was the only nurse killed by enemy action throughout the war–ironically in Cabot Strait.

The Germans won the battle of the St. Lawrence, at least temporarily. The great ports of

Card sharks and mouth-organ minstrels huddle together in cramped quarters belowdecks. Much has been written about the camaraderie of troops, but feuds and fistfights were also common.

Montreal and Quebec were the best equipped for loading cargo and had the fastest turn-around time. But the navy was not able to protect them, and sailings from the St. Lawrence ports were temporarily discontinued. Twenty-three Allied ships were sunk in the river and the gulf, and 700 lives were lost.

invasion of Normandy

The St. Lawrence and western Atlantic were not the only theatres of the war for the RCN. Canadian sailors saw action from the Aleutians to Manzanillo, Mexico, from the Bay of Biscay to Beirut. On the perilous Murmansk convoy route, a hockey team from the destroyer *Algonquin* played against a Russian team in the port of Murmansk and lost. Canadian ships took part in every seaborne invasion of the war in Europe, helping cover the invasion of North Africa and mine-sweeping a path ahead of the mighty invasion of Normandy. No fewer than a hundred Canadian warships and dozens of landing craft took part in the Normandy landing. Two former CN passenger ships, the *Prince Henry* and *Prince David*, played major roles as infantry landing ships in the invasion of the south of France and the invasion of Greece. During the liberation of Athens, bearded, sun-bronzed Canadian petty officers danced with Greek men on the docks at Piraeus and next day staggered up the Acropolis, ouzo oozing from every pore.

The pride of the RCN was four powerful "Tribal Class" destroyers, the *Haida*, the *Huron*, the *Athabaskan* and the *Iroquois*. They were part of the famous 10th Destroyer Squadron of the Royal Navy at Plymouth and fought German destroyers off the French coast. When the *Athabaskan* was sunk in one such action, the *Haida* skipper, Commander Harry DeWolf, chased the German destroyer like an avenging angel, pouring shell after shell into it and driving it onto the beach, a blazing wreck. He then returned to pick up survivors from the *Athabaskan* under the guns of enemy shore batteries.

But the "cockle shell heroes" of the Motor Torpedo Boat flotillas were the most glamourous men in the navy. Like the American PT-boats, these seventy-foot MTBS were the fastest navy ships afloat. Their skippers were men from the navy volunteer reserve who had learned their trade skimming over the midnight waters of the Muskoka Lakes, Lac St. Louis and Georgian Bay.

With three 1,500 horsepower marine engines and 7,000 gallons of highly flammable octane gas in the tanks, flotillas of MTBS zipped across the calm night seas, fifty yards apart, at speeds up to forty-two knots. They attacked enemy coastal convoys, fought heavily-armed flak trawlers and engaged in brief battles with E-boats. Veteran skipper Tony Law, a Quebec City artist who led the Canadian 29th Flotilla, once roared out of Dover to do David-and-Goliath battle with two escaping German battle cruisers. Toronto yachtsman Charles "Bones" Burk earned a measure of fame when, too close to fire torpedoes, he physically manhandled a depth charge over the side of his boat under the bows of an enemy merchantman to blow it up.

"Pirates of the Adriatic"

The most flamboyant of the MTB skippers was Lieutenant Commander Tom Fuller, who with his "Pirates of the Adriatic" was a legend in every Mediterranean port. Born with the heart of a privateer, Fuller captured his first ship, a thirty-ton schooner laden with explosives, early in April 1944. Two nights later he and his men boarded two more armed schooners and towed their prizes back to base with eleven German prisoners. Gradually mock-piracy took firmer hold among his crew members, and they took to wearing gold earrings and gaudy bandanas, and swarmed over gunwales brandishing regulation navy cutlasses. Every other night that summer Fuller's pirates met with success, sinking ships and capturing I-boats crowded with three or four dozen German soldiers. If the admiralty frowned on his bizarre methods, it beamed at his results.

Fuller's triumphs reached their climax late in July when three of his MTBS engaged a superior enemy force. They damaged three E-boats so severely they were sunk by aircraft the following day. They took sixty-five German troops prisoner; they sank two I-boats and the 400-ton schooner, *Vega*. A star shell intended to light up the night sky fell by chance into a bucket of gasoline on the decks of the *Vega*, setting it afire. In his official report Fuller noted: "It is regretted that the prize could not be brought in. She contained several tons of German beer as well as field guns."

vital cargo

It was fitting that the Royal Canadian Navy could boast the likes of Tom Fuller. In six years it had grown from an insignificant fleet to the third largest Allied navy, with close to four hundred ships at sea. Personnel increased fifty-fold, to 100,000, of whom 5,000 were the valuable women of the "Wrens."

Through the long years at sea, the RCN escorted over 25,000 Allied merchant ships safely across the North Atlantic. In their holds and tanks or lashed to their decks were millions of tons of vital cargo: oil and gas, guns and butter, aircraft and armoured cars, grain, flour, cheese, bacon, apples, steel and timber, millions of Sweet Caporal and Macdonald's Export cigarettes at special prices (300 for $1) and thousands of cases of Dawes' Black Horse Ale in white quart bottles from Montreal – the brew prized above all others in many Mediterranean ports.

"Now remember—this alarm is only to be given if we are invaded."

By the summer of '42 the Battle of the Atlantic reached Canadian coastal and inland waters, as far as Anticosti Island. Amidst the public's hue and cry for truth about German landings, Maclean's *cartoonist Salo Roth drew this.*

Although Canada was not a party to the 1943 Quebec Conference, PM *Mackenzie King managed to appear in all the photographs. He told his diary: "My own feeling is that Churchill and Roosevelt being at Quebec, and myself acting as host, will be quite sufficient to make clear that all three are in conference together."*

CHAPTER FIVE

Canada Carries On

It's incredible that one should have such a dramatic view of a battle, and on such a gorgeous warm day . . . War on such a day seems particularly tragic.

Matthew Halton, CBC broadcast, Dec. 8, 1943

"You fellows in Sorel who make these twenty-five-pounders, listen to them now in action!" It was CBC war correspondent Marcel Ouimet speaking from somewhere in Italy. He had set up his mobile sound equipment on the high ground between the German and Canadian lines. As two thousand guns spoke, he opened his microphone. He was addressing the listeners back home in Quebec who had made the explosives.

Keeping up morale on the home front was vital. So was the need for eye-witness news from the battlefront, most of the war being fought an ocean away, in countries few Canadians had seen and in towns many had never heard of. The task of bringing the war home to Canadians fell naturally enough to an intrepid band of radio commentators, newspaper correspondents, photographers and artists, some of whom faced as much danger in their line of duty as the men in the front lines.

The major source of information was radio. As the battlefronts sprouted, major newspapers printed maps of each new battle zone, to be cut out and pinned up in the kitchen or living room next to the radio. Twice a day 1.8 million Canadians listened as the sound of Big Ben booming from the clock tower at Westminster announced the start of the BBC overseas news. On January 1, 1941, the CBC introduced its own National News, with a tall, young Ottawa native named Lorne Greene as its first announcer. His resonant voice which suited the succession of Allied set-backs soon earned him the nickname, the "Voice of Doom." Two years later, as the tide began to turn, Greene was replaced by the more spirited Earl Cameron.

The war years marked the golden age of CBC radio. The first Canadian troop convoy to Britain sailed with a sound engineer in its midst. Before he left Toronto with the CBC's No. 1 Overseas Unit, Art Holmes scrounged an armoured truck from the army and outfitted it with the cumbersome sound and record cutting equipment necessary in the years before magnetic tape and transistors. During the London blitz, as night after night the *Luftwaffe* tried to bomb the British capital into submission, Holmes scorned the safety of air raid shelters and wheeled his mobile recording van out to Hyde Park, down to the docks, and all over the city of London, recording the wail of air raid sirens, the awesome drone of approaching German bomber squadrons, the crackle of anti-aircraft batteries and the ominous swish of land mines as they drifted down on their small parachutes.

Until then it was fashionable for radio commentators to talk incessantly over whatever event

Over a million daily listeners and a thousand fan letters a week kept The Happy Gang at the top of radio ratings throughout the war years.

they were covering. This new blend of actual sound effects interspersed with commentary was the hallmark of the CBC's contribution to the art of reporting. Later Holmes' unique library of sounds was used time and again in documentaries and Hollywood war movies.

One night as German bombers dropped high explosives and incendiaries on London, Ernie Bushnell accompanied Art Holmes on his nightly sortie. Bushnell was a CBC colleague, on loan to the BBC to run its North American service. In the confusion, amid the crumbling buildings, the injured and the fires, the pair spied a little old lady indomitably serving cups of tea to air raid wardens, firemen and rescue workers from her front doorstep. Bushnell had been trying, without success, to persuade horrified BBC chiefs to do a soap opera about the war. That little old lady became the inspiration for "Front Line Family," a family saga that played for years in Britain, Canada and the United States.

For the envied positions as war correspondents, the big daily newspapers and weekly magazines selected their top men. They were in a league of their own. The grand old man of the group was the *Star Weekly*'s Greg Clark, a cagey leprechaun of a man who had emerged from the trenches of World War I with a major's crown on his epaulettes and a Military Cross on his tunic. Fellow war correspondent Doug Amaron once said of Clark: "He reduces everything to its most human denominator." The Montreal *Standard* sent Lionel Shapiro, who would stand amid the clatter of a makeshift press room somewhere in Europe and cheerfully claim: "I've just written the greatest story . . . . " From the Winnipeg *Free Press* came J.A.M. Cook, who wrote this sardonic lead for his story on the historic D-Day landings:

This morning there landed on the beaches of Normandy tens of thousands of men, thousands of armoured cars, hundreds of tanks. There were Bren-gun carriers by the score, artillery pieces by the hundreds. But not a single horse. What on earth happened to the horse in warfare?

One byline that was familiar to every newspaper reader in Canada belonged to Ross Munro, one of the top Allied correspondents. The invasion of Sicily was the biggest news of 1943, and Ross Munro broke the story seven hours ahead of anyone else in the world.

Munro had waded ashore with the Canadian troops and watched them storm inland. He perched his waterproof portable typewriter on the beach and tapped out his story, then sent it to a Canadian ship offshore, where the wireless operator would transmit it to the military censors at Allied headquarters in Algiers. The censors were to delete any details they didn't want the Germans to know and hold it until the high command was ready to announce the momentous invasion. But an RAF wireless operator on Malta who was tuned to the same frequency intercepted the message and relayed it direct to its final address: Canadian Press, London.

The Allied commanders were furious and threatened to banish him from the theatres of war. But when tempers cooled Ross Munro was allowed to rejoin the crew of Canadian war correspondents who followed the troops through Italy, France and northwest Europe. They lived together in caves, gutted farmhouses, empty hotels and occasionally splendid villas, boasting about their stories and bitching about the censors.

Of the "Warcos" Ralph Allen was one of the best. A red-haired *Globe and Mail* sports writer from Oxbow, Saskatchewan, Allen preferred bilious yellow corduroys to the regulation khaki and common foot soldiers to brasshats. This is an excerpt from his account of the liberation of Paris:

Paris today is Betty Grable on a bicycle and Billy the Kid on a bender. Paris is the Mona Lisa in a jeep and

The Maple Leaf

"HANG ON TO THE CAT, WE'LL TEST THIS ONE NEXT."

"WHAT I WANT TO GIT MOST OUT OF THIS WAR .. IS ME!"

YOU SCRAM! THERE AINT ROOM FOR THREE HERE."

CHRISTMAS PREPARATIONS—A LA MODE.

The first issue of The Maple Leaf *rolled off the press in Naples on "borrowed or stolen" paper, and from then on was "one of the three M's in a soldier's life–Meals, Mail and* Maple Leaf.*" Staff included Bing Coughlin, creator of "Herbie"; "Monty and Johnny" cartoonist Les Callan; and Ted "The Moaner" Reeve.*

TUNE IN TONIGHT!

Borden's "Canadian Cavalcade"

CFRB

TORONTO

9.30 - 10.00 P.M.

Dramatic episodes from the lives of heroes and heroines on the home and fighting fronts.

Presented by
The Borden Company Limited

Wartime radio was a melange of dramatized true-life hero stories, soap operas like "Soldier's Wife," and commercially sponsored variety programmes. Borden's "Canadian Cavalcade" featured announcer Lorne Greene, nicknamed "The Voice of Doom" for his resonant readings of tragic news stories.

Clean clothes at any cost! This "automatic wringer-washer," assembled from salvaged parts and pieces found in town, looks like a creation of the madcap American inventor, Rube Goldberg. (Shirts and socks laundered @ 2¢ a mile.)

François Villon behind a Sten gun. Paris is all the people in the world packed into the biggest parade that was ever held. Paris is all the flags and all the singing, all the waves and all the cheers.... I have no hesitancy in admitting I had an anxious hour of ambush in the Rue de Rivoli, and as I sit typing this despatch in a sinfully luxurious suite in the Ritz Hotel, bullets are splattering on the walls of the courtyard not fifty feet away. Like all the shooting in Paris today, there is nothing much you can do about it but ignore it. And besides, as the last incipient movie actress who kissed me (forcibly, honey, I swear) expressed it: "Why let a little shooting spoil a day like this?"

The war correspondents came through largely unscathed, although Gillis Purcell lost a leg when a chute failed to open on paratroop exercises in England early in the war. Sidelined back home, he became general manager of Canadian Press. Combat cameramen and photographers were not so lucky. The army's No. 2 Canadian Film and Photo Unit distinguished itself during the Normandy invasion. Gilbert Milne went in with RCN beach commandoes ahead of the first assault wave to photograph the 3rd Division as it came in. Ken Bell and nine others landed at various points along the beaches. Frank Duberville and Bill Grant rode ashore on top of a self-propelled gun. The photographs and film footage were hustled aboard a fast ship returning to England, arrived hours ahead of any others, and appeared in newspapers and newsreels around the world.

Three weeks later under German mortar fire in Caen, these same men of No. 2 CFPU shot *You Can't Kill a City*, the first documentary film made from a prepared script on an active field of battle. It was written and directed by the commanding

Charles Comfort and many other artists from the Group of Canadian Painters saw the war from behind portable easels. Comfort's earmark was the Canadian "Red Patch" (pages 22 and 24).

Free Press. Before the interview was over, Grierson had hired her to work for the NFB. In her first two days she worked thirty-two hours. In a few short months she made four shorts on the value of vitamins and a film on wartime day nurseries titled *Before They Are Six*.

Aside from being in it, the only place to see the war was at the movies, between the cartoon and the feature presentation. There was a twenty-five per cent Canadian or British content quota. The NFB's best-known production was "Canada Carries On," a series produced for the Wartime Information Board and shown at first once a month, and later twice a month, in nine hundred movie houses across Canada. Each segment was ten to twenty minutes long and featured ordinary Canadians making their own individual contribution to the war effort: a corvette crew on North Atlantic convoy duty, a prairie farmer struggling to bring in the harvest, women rivetting an airplane together in a war plant, an RCAF bomber crew over Berlin.

V for Victory

NFB documentary shorts were startling. They were crisply edited and urgent, many with musical scores by Lucio Agostini and commentaries by the ubiquitous Lorne Greene. Norman McLaren, in the NFB animation department, developed a unique method of drawing directly on film stock. One of his earliest animations was *V for Victory*, celebrating Winston Churchill's famous two-finger symbol. The idea was first suggested to him by the Canadian spymaster, Sir William Stephenson. Other McLaren creations were *Dollar Dance*, which pointed out the evils of wartime inflation, and *5 for 4*, an animation set to boogie-woogie music encouraging the purchase of War Savings Certificates.

To reach farming and small-town communities far from movie theatres, the NFB set up a network

"The Coldcream Guards" tickling the troops' funny bone.

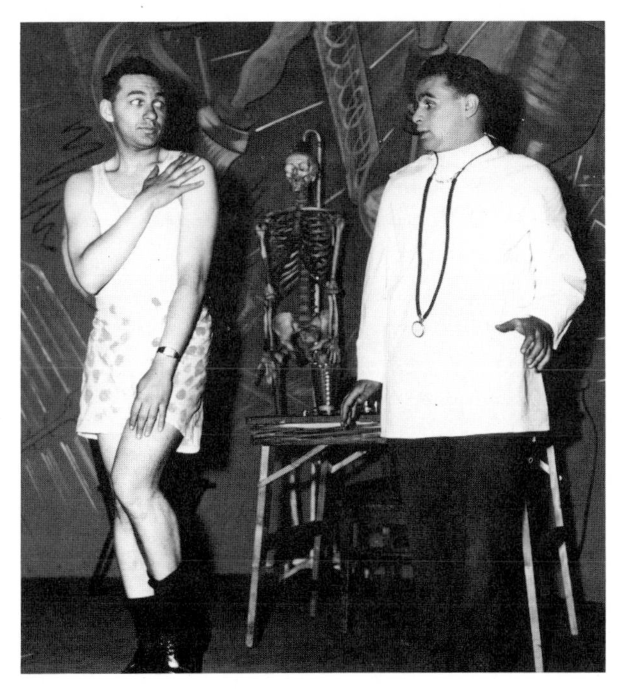

Two familiar faces from the Army Show in Normandy, '44.

Showtime

Slapstick, musical comedy, black humour and Colonel Blimp jokes about the brass were highlights of the Army, Navy and Air Force Shows that toured Canada and military camps overseas. The circuit created its own stars, among them Lt. John Pratt of the 120-member cast of "Meet The Navy," and Sgts. Johnny Wayne and Frank Shuster of the Army Show cast (known unofficially as the "Coldcream Guards"). Unlike WW I shows, many of the performers were "real dames" — CWACs, Wrens and WDs. But even in POW camps, where skits had to be put on "in drag," soldiers found laughter was the best medicine.

These POW *"hoofers" are "camping it up" behind barbed wire in* Stalag XXI's *Christmas revue.*

John Grierson
The Chief of Propaganda

When the National Film Board was created in 1939, its purpose was not art but propaganda. And as its director, John Grierson had the task of keeping public opinion on the right track. Posters, films and photos, all carefully edited, were seen across the country. There was the series, "Canada Carries On" — short documentaries on the home-front effort; the periodical booklet *Canada at War* (see p. 9); and a dazzling array of recruitment and Victory Bond posters. The output of the NFB under Grierson was immense and of top quality by any standard. In 1946, however, his career ended abruptly. Asked to testify at the espionage hearings that followed the Gouzenko revelations, he left the NFB and Canada. He died in 1972.

of forty-seven travelling "theatres." Each consisted of a projectionist and his equipment in a rattletrap wartime automobile, sometimes towing a portable generator behind him, visiting twenty places each month. The intrepid projectionists drove dusty roads and lurched through gumbo mud. In winter, with the wartime shortage of antifreeze, they had to drain their radiators each night and fill them up again next morning with warm water, and sometimes burn oil-soaked sawdust under the engine pan to free the sluggish oil.

The audiences loved the shows. In one New Brunswick community not a single member of the audience had ever seen a motion picture before; at another in British Columbia, no one had seen a "talkie." At Alder Flats in Alberta folks turned out in forty-below (F.) weather to sit in a lumbermen's hall to watch the films. Often the audiences made a night of it and several of the projectionists were in demand as square-dance callers. Others, like Damase Bouvier, staged amateur talent shows after the film, and one night in Morinville, Alberta, Bouvier cut the first disc for a young singer named Robert Goulet.

scads of CWAC *chorines*

The war directly spawned another pleasant evening's entertainment for Canadians. In 1943, "The Army Show" opened its Canadian tour at the Victory Theatre in Toronto, before splitting into five smaller companies to entertain the troops behind the lines throughout Europe. The show had an all-soldier cast, as well trained to shoot a Sten gun as to do a buck and wing. Most of the skits and song lyrics were written by two sergeants, Johnny Wayne and Frank Shuster, who also performed their stunts amidst scads of CWAC chorines. The West created its own army show, "Rodeo Rhythm," directed by Kit Carson, a rancher from Maple Creek, Saskatchewan. Staged under a canvas big-top in England, it featured Private Rita Nadeau from Meadow Lake in a tandem riding act and Private Len Houle of Courtenay, British Columbia, rope-spinning in a white Stetson. The highlight was a spectacular water ballet.

You'll Get Used To It

The navy took the wind out of the army's sails when its show, "Meet the Navy" became a box office hit at London's famous Hippodrome theatre. After the first night Noel Coward wrote: "The impact was quite electrifying . . . . It had freshness and it had clarity, expert singing and dancing and remarkable chorus work." Alan and Blanche Lund were the headline dancers, but most of the 120 naval ratings, officers and Wrens were amateurs. The highlight of the show was Lieutenant John Pratt, a young Montreal architect who shuffled mournfully on stage in size XL blue overalls and a sailor's cap three sizes too small, and sang this ditty:

You'll get used to it, you'll get used to it.
Oh the navy, bless the navy, you'll get used to it.
When you go on leave to find,
That the girl you left behind,
Has been as true in every way,
As you have been to her, I'll say,
It's wonderful, it's marvellous,
How two can always play at every game.
You gotta get used to it and you'll get used to it,
But you better get yourself another dame.

The song had been written two years earlier in an internment camp at Farnham, Quebec, by a young German Jew, jazz pianist Freddie Grant, who was incarcerated there. The lyrics could be varied to suit any wartime context. As well as anything else, the song summed up the attitude, on the battlefront or on the home front, of Canadians carrying on.

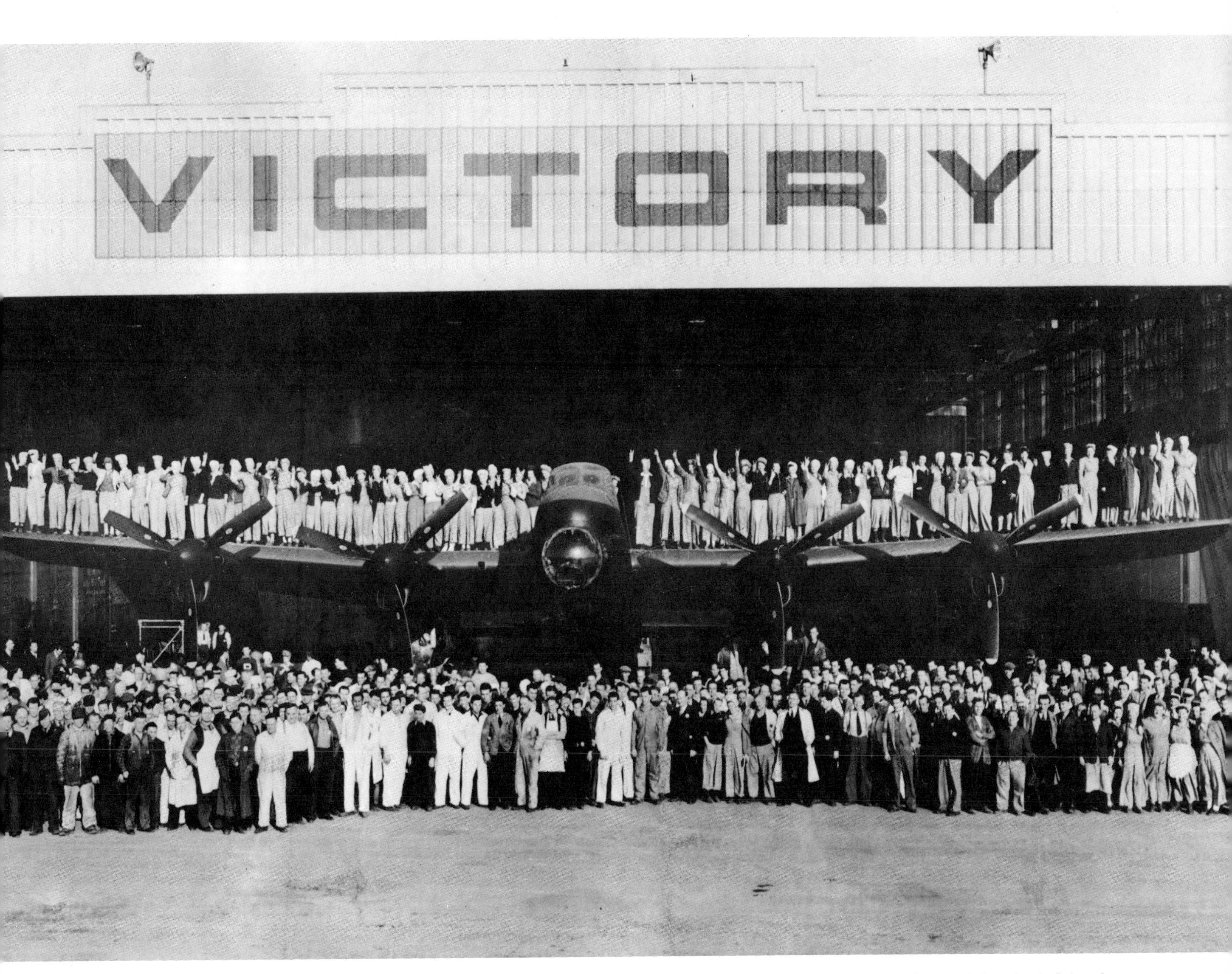

Sixty-five women workers span the 102-foot wings of this Lancaster at Victory Aircraft in Malton, Ontario, celebrating completion of their fortieth bomber.

Propaganda

Nowhere was it clearer than in posters that a picture was worth thousands of words. No one needed to be reminded that the struggle was for hearts and minds at home, as well as for territory abroad. The Wartime Information Board, under the direction of the NFB's John Grierson, spelled out for artists the purposes of propaganda: to instil pride and confidence in Canada and her institutions; to show the consequences of defeat; to create a sense of personal responsibility and an acceptance of the need for sacrifice; and, above all, to build up assurance of victory. Poster appeals were both emotional and intellectual. Those calling for recruits fell barely short of calling the unenlisted cowards. Those selling Victory Bonds almost reached into people's pockets for the $4 minimum purchase. "Loose Talk" posters created the spectre of a spy around every corner, and larger-than-life Nazis and Japs glowered from caricatures. The message in other media was much the same. The CBC brought in Vincent Price, the dean of gothic horror, to narrate a series of spy dramas set in New Brunswick and B.C. towns. British and Hollywood films blended backlot bunker scenes with documentary footage to show Allied heroes and Axis villains. Short stories in magazines all had an underlying message — enlist, save, watch what you're saying.

G. K. Odell's Victory Bond poster is one of the finest Canadian examples of propaganda art. The claws of Nazi and Japanese fascism threaten both mother and child.

In 1944 health officials estimated that over 300,000 Canadians were infected with VD, and under wartime conditions the epidemic was spreading. Every major magazine and newspaper carried articles and ads demystifying the subject: No, you could not pick it up in restaurants and public lavatories; yes, you could from "the casual pickup, professional or amateur prostitute and good-time girl." The poster war reached from the barracks to the bedroom and bordello.

Although the warning in this British poster was directed at servicemen and civilians overseas, its message applied to Canadians as well. In 1945, 9,000 Japanese balloon bombs floated over the Pacific, 80 of them reaching Canada. A group of Alberta schoolboys narrowly missed death when they dismantled one such device with a crude soldering iron. Just south of the border, an Oregon woman and five children were killed when one of the balloon bombs exploded.

Censorship and tight security at military camps and munitions plants would have been powerless against the kind of gossip network imagined by the artist who conceived this poster.

CHAPTER SIX

The Secret War

The Big Lie takes many forms. It can win bloodless victories for Germany if our leaders are soft-headed . . . Germany's final enemies are in North America. Hitler will try first to sap our courage by winning friends there.

William Stephenson in *A Man Called Intrepid*

On Monday morning, November 10, 1942, a thick-set civilian carrying two suitcases checked into Earl Annett's hotel in the small Gaspé town of New Carlisle. Strangers were rare around the Bay of Chaleur in the off-season, and when the newcomer said he had come by bus, the hotel keeper's curiosity turned to suspicion. The bus had arrived some hours earlier. When the stranger came down to lunch, Annett searched his room. The suitcases were locked, but he did find a box of matches from Belgium, a country occupied by the Germans for the past two years. Annett sent his son for the police who promptly arrested the man.

Captain Werner Janowski was a German agent who had landed the night before, rowing ashore from a U-boat in a rubber dinghy. He was under orders to establish a base in Montreal and send information each day by shortwave transmitter to control in the German port of Hamburg. He was also to assist other agents due to arrive later. If he needed help, he was to contact Canadian fascist sympathisers. All this RCMP Inspector Clifford Harvison and Sergeant Pete Bordeleau discovered when they interrogated Janowski the following day.

The *Abwehr*, Germany's intelligence service, had been sloppy in the Janowski operation. It had supplied him with $5,000 in Canadian bills, but some were of a denomination the government had withdrawn from circulation three years earlier. His documents were equally bad: his cover story was that he lived in Toronto, yet his national registration card was a bilingual one issued only to Quebeckers. A trained saboteur who had already won the Iron Cross, Janowski was duped into believing he had been double-crossed by the *Gestapo*, and the RCMP convinced him he should become a double-agent.

With the co-operation of Canadian and British military intelligence, the RCMP went to elaborate lengths to set Janowski up in Montreal. It monitored the broadcasts from Hamburg and fed Janowski suitable replies. Hamburg was interested in port defences on the St. Lawrence, the locations of anti-submarine nets, ship sailings, troop strengths, and details of the secret aircraft, the Mosquito, that was being built in Toronto.

A second German agent landed later on the New Brunswick coast. Although his arrival was undetected, he proved even less loyal to his cause than Janowski. He immediately ditched his transmitter–plainly intending to do no spying–

To Work For Britain

A Department of the British Government in New York City requires several reliable young women, fully competent in secretarial work and of matriculation or better educational standing. The chief need is for expert file clerks and for typists and stenographers able to take one hundred and twenty-five words per minute. Dependable character and satisfactory background essential. Those selected can expect to serve for the duration of the war. Wages and working conditions are good. Travelling expenses to New York will be paid.

APPLY in your own handwriting, stating your age, education and parentage, with full details of your business experience and wages received and enclosing a recent snapshot. Also give two responsible references. Address your application to Box 10[illegible]7 Telegram

AT once,
EXPERIENCED operators
ON ladies' blouses
AND ladies' neckwear.
DRESS ESSENTIALS, Ltd.,
284 KING street west.

Buried in the Toronto Telegram's *want ads section in 1941 was this piece recruiting "secretaries" to work for the British government in New York. Behind the ad was the British Secret Intelligence Service.*

Resignation threats from anti-conscription cabinet ministers on one shore, and military "red tabs" on the other, put Mackenzie King's war policy to the rapids test in November '44.

went to Ottawa and spent his mornings in the Parliamentary library reading the current copies of Hansard, and his afternoons at the movies. When his money ran out, he gave himself up.

Long before war broke out, the RCMP Special Branch had infiltrated and investigated subversive organizations and fifth columnists in Canada, including the Canadian fascists, the Canadian Communist Party, the *Deutschbund* (a German patriotic society that held meetings in swastika-draped halls in some Prairie towns), and the Ku Klux Klan. The office of the German State Railway in Dominion Square, Montreal, was a centre for Nazi agents. Others masqueraded as importers, engineers and businessmen. In the forty-eight hours after Canada declared war, the RCMP Special Branch arrested and interned 250 suspected Nazis in Quebec alone, most of them in Montreal, and comparable numbers in other big cities. The apparatus of German espionage was quickly shattered. When Mussolini threw in with Hitler in June 1940, there was a similarly swift round-up of allegedly dangerous Italians.

internment camp

Until June 1940 the Canadian fascist party had been allowed to function. Its leader, Adrien Arcand, forty-one years old, was a tall Montrealer of fiery eloquence. He claimed 12,000 members, issued his own money, (to be redeemed after he became dictator of Canada), and campaigned on an anti-Communist, anti-Semitic, pro-Catholic, pro-French-Canadian platform. In 1940 Arcand and his ten lieutenants were arrested and sent to internment camps. Six leaders who took their places were also interned.

That same summer, the colourful and popular mayor of Montreal, Camillien Houde, spoke out to young Quebec men, advising them not to take part in the compulsory National Registration. One night, after working late as he often did, Houde left the Hôtel-de-Ville shortly before midnight, attired as usual in his swallowtail coat, striped pants, spats, cravat, top hat and carrying his cane. The RCMP were waiting on the hotel steps. They arrested him for sedition and whisked him off by car to an internment camp outside Petawawa. There he worked as a woodcutter for twenty cents a day instead of his annual mayor's salary of $20,000, and in his four-year confinement sweated off a hundred pounds. After his release he was promptly re-elected mayor of Montreal.

Racial and religious discrimination was commonplace in Canada during the forties. There was far less animosity toward German-Canadians than there had been in the earlier war. But Colonel C.P. Stacey, a military historian, records that in the early months of the war some regimental recruiting officers sought to dissuade qualified Jews from seeking to become officers on the grounds that Christian troops would not follow them into battle. In July 1940, Jehovah's Witnesses were declared illegal and their magazines were confiscated. Like the Quakers, Doukhobors, Hutterites and Mennonites, they were pacifists.

deceit and dirty tricks

Canada was not immune to the paranoia of war, and rumours of spies and fifth columnists flourished, most of them baseless. The triumph of the understaffed and overworked RCMP stymied subversive activities so successfully that no significant acts of enemy sabotage took place in Canada during the war. Still, a secret war of espionage, counter-intelligence, deceit and dirty tricks, of assassinations, ruined reputations, faked letters and seduction to gain enemy codes and ciphers was well-based in Canada. And the propaganda war, only slightly more out in the open, was part of it.

The great goal of the secret war in 1940 and 1941 was to enlist the active support of the United States, still strongly isolationist and the most powerful neutral nation on earth. Nazi agents and propagandists thronged Washington, New York and Chicago, stirring up pro-German and anti-British feelings. Among their supporters were the highly vocal, right wing America Firsters who were so anti-Semitic they refused to sing "God Bless America" in Madison Square Garden because the composer, Irving Berlin, was a Jew.

"no U.S. entanglement"

One of the most outspoken fascist sympathizers was Father Charles Coughlin, an ex-Canadian born in Hamilton and educated at the University of Toronto. Father Coughlin, pastor of the Church of the Little Flower in suburban Detroit, had gathered a great following in the thirties as the "Radio Priest." He was finally silenced in 1942 when his magazine, *Social Justice*, was banned under the American Espionage Act.

As early as February 1940, *Maclean's* magazine reported:

Canada's tourist trade is shrinking because of rumours spread by German agents in the U.S. They say that in the stress of war, Canadians do not welcome American tourists; that Canadian authorities are seizing cars brought in by tourists and the government is taking all U.S. money entering the country and giving only 59 cents on the dollar in return.

These rumours were unfounded, but damaging nevertheless. Canada needed scarce American dollars to buy machinery and war materials from the United States.

Republican presidential candidate Wendell Willkie campaigned that election year of 1940 on a platform of "No U.S. entanglement in European wars." Among the newspapermen aboard his campaign train, whistle-stopping across the United

Camillien Houde
Le Maire Populaire

When Ottawa announced conscription of eligible men for home service in the summer of 1940, some Canadians, including Montreal mayor Camillien Houde, saw the act as a prelude to the country's further entanglement in "Britain's war." When, at a public rally, he urged Québecois not to register, he was arrested. The federal authorities, fearing a backlash, tried to suppress news of the incident; but to English Canada's surprise, both *Le Devoir* and *La Presse* felt Houde was carrying his nationalism a bit too far, and went as far as calling him "a fool who got what he deserved." In 1944 the portly ex-mayor was released and returned to Montreal amidst great fanfare. He was back in the mayor's office with the first election, and stayed there until retirement in 1954.

Separated from their families, these men wait to hear which work camp is their destination.

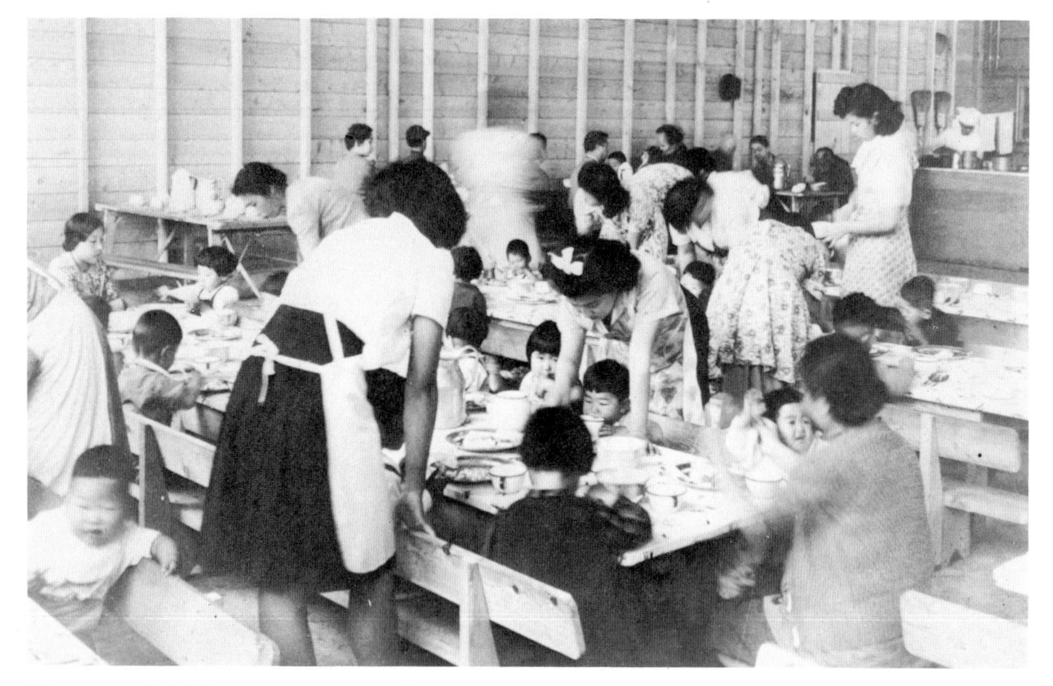

Women and children were temporarily housed in draughty exhibition buildings in Vancouver.

The Enemy Within

December 7, 1941 — Pearl Harbor: it seemed to take just one event to make Canadians forget that they were fighting a war to safeguard the ideals of democracy. Within days, 38 Japanese-Canadians were arrested as subversives, detained and sent to prison camps. All persons, whether native-born or naturalized citizens, or landed immigrants, were fingerprinted and issued identification cards. Fishermen had their boats impounded, farmers and shopkeepers had their land and property confiscated, and over 20,000 people were shipped to makeshift relocation camps in the interior. Run-down, ghost-town miners' cabins became their homes for three years, where they tried to educate their children, tend their gardens and create some sort of life for themselves. They had no rights, no privileges, no privacy. The tragedy of it all was that few voices rose in protest, and those that did were lost in the din of war and racist propaganda. "Look behind the solicitor for a CCF candidate, and you will see an Oriental leering over his shoulder with an eye on you and your daughter. . . ." was the message of one Liberal candidate's radio ad. On a city street, an Oriental woman was seen wearing the placard: "I am Chinese, *not* Japanese." When the war was over and the government made a lame attempt to blot out this national disgrace, those who were lucky received about a quarter of the real value of their property, and a debt of bitterness was the nation's legacy.

"For reasons of national security," almost 13,000 citizens of Japanese origin were herded onto trucks and buses and sent to "relocation camps."

Students at Queen Mary School in North Vancouver prepare for an air raid drill, strapping on masks for a make-believe Japanese gas attack. On the night of June 20, 1942, a submarine lobbed a few shells at Estevan Point on Vancouver Island, and although there was no damage done, the war had reached Canada.

States, was Bruce Hutchison of the Vancouver *Sun*, a bemused and somewhat reluctant Canadian agent. Armed with a princely $5,000 in expense money, Hutchison's real assignment was to visit publishers and editors in every city to inform them of Canada's war effort and convince them of the rightness of the cause. Although President Roosevelt and millions of ordinary Americans were sympathetic to Canada and Britain, political realities demanded continued neutrality.

Meanwhile, the Nazis held victory banquets in swank Manhattan hotels. Attending were business leaders who thought Britain was finished anyway, who admired Hitler for kicking the Commies out of Germany, and who wanted to do business with the Germans. Into this scene in 1940 moved a quiet Canadian who leased two floors of the Rockefeller Center in New York for a modest organization called British Security Co-ordination, or BSC. His name was William Stephenson.

"Intrepid"

An orphaned Manitoba farm boy with a passion for the new-fangled wireless, Stephenson had, in his first twenty years, done more than most men would in a lifetime. Badly gassed in the trenches of World War I, he had become a crack fighter ace whose reports on the future of aerial warfare had brought him to the attention of the head of British Intelligence. He had invented the wirephoto machine for transmitting photographs vast distances, dabbled in television, and had become a millionaire industrialist in Britain. He was to become, under the code name "Intrepid," the greatest spymaster of the Western Hemisphere and a confidential emissary between Winston Churchill and Franklin D. Roosevelt.

Directing a huge spy network inside a neutral country was a dicey operation. Stephenson relied heavily on Canada for his staff and his training bases. Elaine Knight, a young university graduate from Cornwall, Ontario, was one of more than 750 Canadian women engaged for the duration of the war to work as secretaries and aides at Rockefeller Center and other locations in New York. She worked in one small section recruiting and training Yugoslav immigrants to help Marshal Tito's partisans in the mountains of Dalmatia.

Camp X

Another of the Canadians who worked for the BSC was Tom Drew-Brook, a Toronto stockbroker who headed that city's Station M. Station M specialized in technical wizardry. The staff located old European typewriters and bond paper on which to prepare incriminating letters and necessary documents for agents. They gathered old European clothing for agents to wear, and canvassed recent immigrants for telltale European objects to lend the agents authenticity.

A weathered farmhouse on Ontario's lakeshore near Oshawa is all that has ever been revealed of Camp X, a major training base for BSC agents and saboteurs. Its secluded location made it ideal for ferrying personnel surreptitiously back and forth from New York State, and traffic was considerable, including FBI director J. Edgar Hoover. Commander Ian Fleming, who later wrote the James Bond spy novels, trained there. Gladstone Murray, the general manager of the CBC, was a member of Stephenson's vast spy network and set up powerful radio transmitters at Camp X which could reach every part of Europe.

At times the camp resembled a Hollywood backlot. Hungarian film producers and directors, Alexander and Zoltan Korda, built models there of Hitler's headquarters in Berlin. Countless young men and women who trained in the devious arts of underwater sabotage, killing and espionage at Camp X landed in Europe. Many did not return.

William Stephenson "Intrepid"

"I am quite certain that your contribution will be among the foremost in having brought victory," FBI director J. Edgar Hoover wrote to William Stephenson. "Wild Bill" Donovan, U.S. head of Strategic Services, said he "taught us all we ever knew about foreign intelligence." And one of his employees called him the only man to enjoy "the unqualified confidence of both Churchill and Roosevelt." William Stephenson was born near Winnipeg in 1896, and served as a fighter pilot in WW I. He scored 20 kills before being shot down, and spent the rest of the war in prison camp. In business in England, he made a fortune in aircraft, cement and steel, and invented the apparatus for transmitting the world's first wire-photo in 1926. In 1940 he was appointed head of British Security Coordination, and under the codename INTREPID directed Allied intelligence and espionage activities.

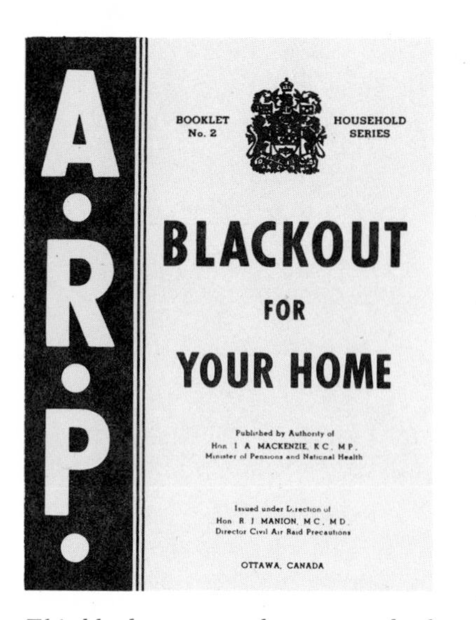

This blackout manual was a standard reference for air raid wardens and the public, especially those on the Pacific. Vancouverites drew their blinds, painted over car headlights, and doused streetlamps for three nights in a row on December 8, 9 and 10 in 1941, after the attack on Pearl Harbor by the Japanese.

Some two dozen Canadians, the majority of them French, joined British Intelligence and were dropped into occupied France. Some operated effectively for months, others parachuted to certain death because their underground units had already been captured by the Gestapo. Among the casualties were three Canadians in their twenties: Frank Pickersgill, a former Sorbonne student; John Macalister, a Rhodes scholar; and Roméo Sabourin, a radio operator from Quebec. After months of interrogation and torture, the three were marched to their execution in September 1944, hanged on hooks in a bare barracks. As they were led away, they sang a ragged chorus of "Alouette."

iron discipline

Enemy agents captured in Canada fared much better. So did 35,000 German prisoners of war shipped here for safekeeping. They lived in special camps in isolated parts of the northern bush or on the prairies and worked in the sugar beet fields and logging camps. The Veterans' Guard of Canada, old sweats from WW I, stood guard over them.

There were quite a number of escapes, although with the cold in winter and the black flies in summer the prisoners seldom got very far. Twenty-eight prisoners escaped once from a camp at Peninsula in northern Ontario. Two were shot and killed in a railroad hut, and the others were soon recaptured. Baron Franz von Werra, a young *Luftwaffe* pilot, jumped from a train outside Smiths Falls, Ontario, made his way to the St. Lawrence River at Prescott and crossed into the neutral United States. But his luck did not hold. Shortly after he reached Germany, he was killed in action.

Within the camps, the *Gestapo* and *SS* exercised their own iron discipline on those who doubted victory for Hitler. At Camp 132 in Medicine Hat, which held 12,000 prisoners, Sgt. Karl Lehmann was beaten and strangled by fellow prisoners. Internees were tried for murder and hanged at Lethbridge in 1946.

POW camps at Lethbridge and Medicine Hat each cost $2 million to build. They were outfitted with modern hospitals, hot and cold running water, showers, playing fields, and recreation rooms large enough for prison symphony orchestras. The camps were far better, many of the prisoners said, than their own barracks back home.

Pearl Harbor and the aftermath

The Japanese attack on Pearl Harbor in December 1941, shocked and frightened British Columbians almost to the point of hysteria. They demanded and received thousands of troops for protection, although the military chiefs in Ottawa never considered a Japanese seaborne invasion as a serious possibility. A solitary Japanese submarine, *I-26*, did surface off the west coast of Vancouver Island many months later. Possibly out of sheer boredom, or a taste for some target practice, it fired a salvo of shells at the lighthouse and wireless station on remote Estevan Point. It did little damage and injured no one.

Once Canada and Japan were at war, however, the RCMP arrested thirty Japanese whom they considered potentially dangerous. The navy confiscated 1,200 Japanese-Canadian fishing boats all the way from Prince Rupert to the Fraser River delta and towed them all to Vancouver. They were eventually sold to Canadians.

But British Columbians – with a history of racial dislike of Orientals – were not appeased. Liberal and Conservative MPs mounted a public campaign to have all 21,000 of B.C.'s Japanese-Canadians removed from a hundred-mile-deep defence zone along the coast. Restrictions on their freedom gradually increased. The government imposed a curfew, banned newspapers, confiscated their automobiles, barred them from schools and expelled sixty of them from the University of British Columbia. Finally, bowing to local pressure, the Canadian government ordered their removal.

Their homes, their land, their businesses, their furniture, most of their possessions – the government confiscated them all and sold them at fire sale prices. They were housed in cow barns at the Pacific National Exhibition grounds in Vancouver until preparations for the exodus were complete. They were allowed to take 150 pounds of clothing, bedding and cooking utensils for each adult, and half as much for children. In the summer of 1942 the majority of them boarded trains for six old ghost towns in the British Columbia interior.

a few empty saloons

At places like Slocan and Greenwood, they found a few empty saloons and hotels and a rash of crude three-room houses measuring fourteen by twenty-four feet, which several families were expected to share. Here they made a new life as best they could.

Of their numbers, 13,000 were native-born Canadians and 3,000 more were naturalized citizens, all deprived of the freedoms and rights guaranteed by law. Several hundred crossed the Rockies to work as farm labourers in the irrigation lands of southern Alberta, the beetfields of Manitoba and the orchards of Ontario. They were seldom welcome on the streets of nearby towns.

Clamour for the deportation of all Japanese-Canadians, regardless of citizenship, continued in British Columbia after the war and the government repatriated 4,000 to Japan before halting the operation. The ghost-town detention camps ceased operation in 1947, and the following year Japanese-Canadians won the right to vote in federal elections.

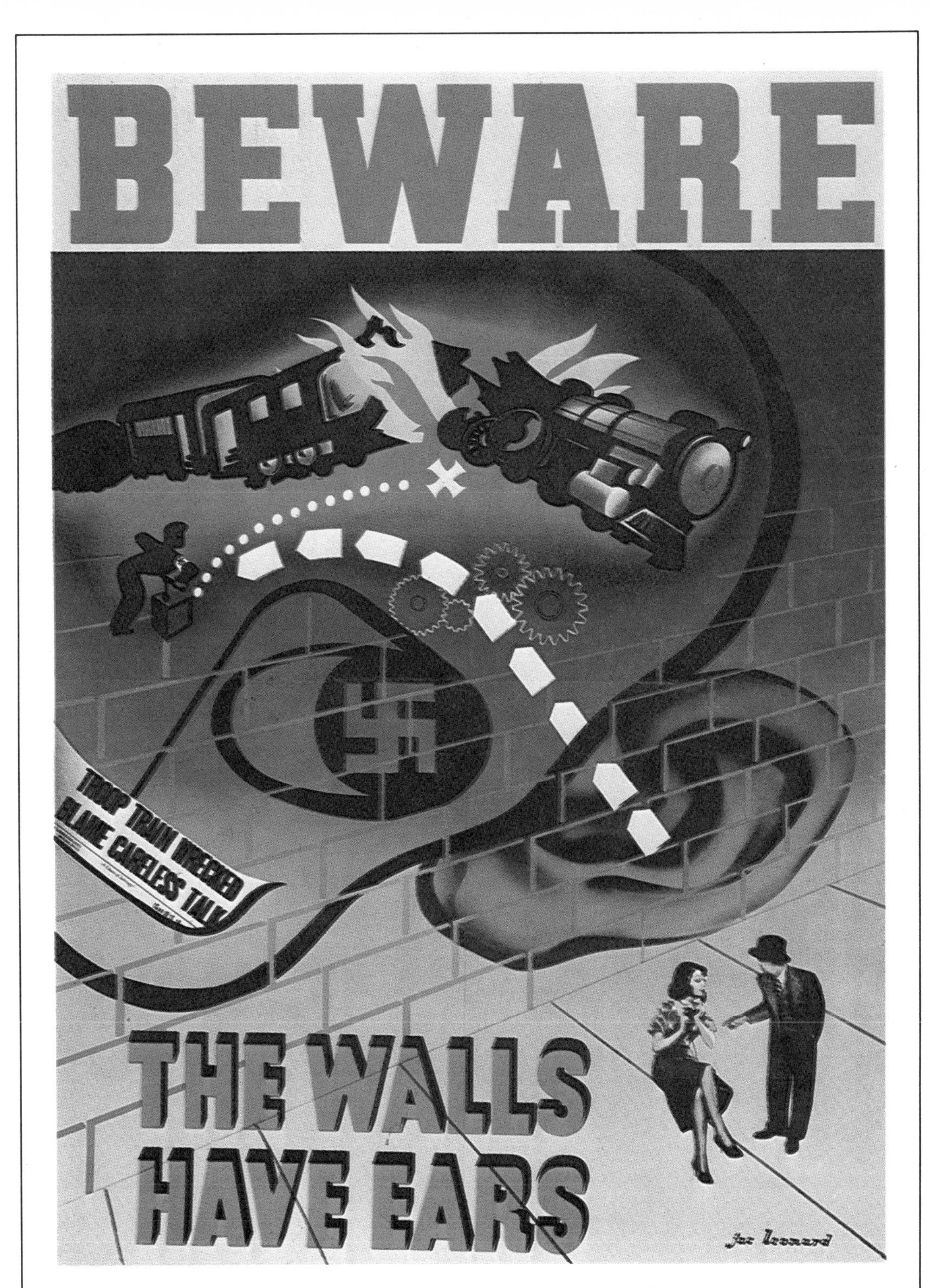

Only two incidents of suspected sabotage in Canada have been revealed, but in Europe at least 28 Canadians worked as special agents behind enemy lines, organizing the resistance, blowing up troop trains, and transmitting coded information. Few, if any, came back alive.

"Entertaining Soldiers" was one of the features in the Christmas issue of Chatelaine *in 1940.*

Magazines of the Forties

Canadians had their choice of magazines in the forties, but in content most articles and ads were much the same. The fashion-conscious looked at "Will the War Affect Fashion," and realized it already had. For wives and sweethearts with men overseas, a short story like "Remembering You" could pack enough emotion for a good cry. "On the Kitchen Front," one of the regular features in *National Home Monthly,* taught cooks how to make do with meatless meals, and Lotta Dempsey's piece, "You'll Be So Nice To Come Home To," gave tips on writing happy letters to the front. Sandwiched between the articles, ads followed the same line of copy: hands rough and red from war work were transformed with a drop of Jergen's lotion; men in restyled old suits ("victory suits") exhorted others to join the "thrift column" and overhaul the wife's old sewing machine; and Holeproof Hosiery apologized for not producing silk and nylon stockings. Post-war articles and ads worried about a possible depression, rising divorce rates, refugees, repatriation and shortages. When rumours of spies were in the wind in late-1945, an instant short story titled "Soviet Steno" appeared in the pages of *Chatelaine*.

General Motors' ad in La Revue Populaire *carried the line,* "La victoire est notre affaire."

"Crisis in Quebec", "How Long Will Japan Last?"

Welcome relief a month after VJ Day — football.

TAMBLYN
FISHERS
NO LEFT TURN

CHAPTER SEVEN

The Repats Return

Victory would not bring back my husband or thousands of other men who had given their lives. Victory would not restore sight to the blind or health to shattered bodies. Victory would not wipe out the memory of horrors from children's minds. But at least the world would have a chance to recover sanity; if people worked as hard for peace as they had for war, some good might be accomplished . . .

Jean Ellis, *Face Powder and Gun Powder* (1947)

On Tuesday, May 1, 1945, as thousands of Canadians sat at the supper table, the news came over the BBC shortwave network that the Russian army was in Berlin and Hitler had committed suicide in his underground bunker. The BBC announcer ended with a line from *Richard III*: "The day is ours. The bloody dog is dead."

Victory in Europe was certain. Two days later this notice appeared in the Winnipeg *Tribune*:

Immediately the proclamation of VE Day is received, all government liquor stores and all beer parlours in Manitoba will be closed. They will be closed the following day.

Other provincial liquor control boards followed suit. There was going to be no unseemly revelry in Canada as six years of war came to an end.

VE Day was set for May 8, but people couldn't wait. On May 7, the Toronto *Telegram* reported:

Before ten o'clock this morning, people were streaming out of offices on Bay Street, hatless and coatless, to celebrate the unconditional surrender of Germany in a blizzard of paper, streamers and confetti.

When the lights went on again all over London that night, Canadian troops on leave joined milling crowds, singing and swaying, dancing and kissing, in Trafalgar Square, in Piccadilly Circus, in crowded pubs all over England.

The same evening in Halifax, naval ratings poured out of the dockyard gates on shore leave. There is seldom much love lost between the solid citizens and the sailors in any large naval port. In Halifax the sailors particularly resented the elders of Fort Massey Church who had forced the closure of the popular Ajax Club for seamen because they objected to sailors drinking beer in their church. On this night crowds of servicemen and women, merchant seamen, dockyard workers and other civilians milled around, looking for some way to celebrate in the grim, grey port. A group of sailors commandeered a streetcar, derailed it and set it alight. Then the growing crowd surged along Barrington Street to two shuttered liquor stores which they broke into and looted, swigging bottles of rum and stuffing mickeys of rye into their jumpers.

Winnipeg's Elmer McKnight penned this song in a Japanese POW camp and somehow convinced his captors to broadcast it over Radio Tokyo. The music was arranged by Freddie Grant, a German Jew interned in a Canadian POW camp during the war.

Opposite page: *Adding machine tape, toilet paper, leaflets and confetti blizzard down from Sparks Street office windows, as civil servants whoop it up on VE Day in Ottawa.*

IT'S ALL OVER! *reads the headline of* Maple Leaf, *but for most troops in Europe and England it would be months before troop ships would be available to carry them back to Canada.*

Next afternoon, the VE Day "celebration" grew uglier. On the garrison sports grounds behind Citadel Hill where the official celebration was in progress, bands played, dignitaries made speeches and clergymen delivered invocations. But 9,000 sailors who had come ashore were in a darker mood. Joined by city rowdies, they proceeded to take the downtown shopping district apart, ripping down victory flags, smashing shop windows and looting stores, while others made love on the grassy slopes. Eventually, as the riot dissipated itself, most of the sailors staggered back to their ships. Stragglers were arrested, and some of the navy men later received prison terms of up to fifteen years for their actions.

In a short while, however, the damage was repaired, the glass was swept up, and the first troopships steamed into Halifax harbour, their decks crowded with thousands of "Repats." Some cheered and waved, others were grimly silent. These men had been the first to sail away to war sixty-eight months earlier, and so they were the first coming home. Meanwhile, in repatriation camps in Britain and Holland, other troops sat and fretted. There was a serious shortage of liners and troopships to bring them home.

VJ Day

One thing was certain: World War II was over for all Canadians in uniform. A month before VE Day, the prime minister had announced that no Canadian would be ordered to the Pacific to fight the Japanese, and that those who did re-volunteer would first be returned to Canada for thirty days leave. Eighty thousand soldiers and small contingents of sailors and airmen did re-volunteer, but very few were ever sent. The new cruiser HMCS *Uganda* was already in the Pacific. The captain wanted to stay, but the crew voted sixty per cent in favour of returning to Esquimalt, where they could exercise their right to discharge or re-volunteer.

Apart from the two battalions sent to Hong Kong and the RCAF squadrons in Burma, Canadians had played little part in the war with Japan. When VJ Day came on August 15, it was an anti-climax for many people, an excuse for a party and for another riot – this time in Sudbury by hard rock miners who had worked underground mining nickel, unable to quit because they were essential war workers, and who now shared neither the glory nor the rewards enjoyed by veterans.

the difficult transition

For the Repats the rewards were as generous as those offered by any of the Allied countries. Concerned about a postwar recession and urged on by the Canadian Legion and editorial writers, the government created the Department of Veterans' Affairs and passed a variety of legislation designed to smooth the difficult transition from the armed forces to civilian life.

The transitions clearly were not easy for many men. They had lived in a world filled with action and fear. They had been fed and clothed. They had given orders or taken them. They had witnessed barbarous scenes. Wide gulfs had separated them from their families and from those who had never seen the war first hand.

Gratuities were $7.50 for each month of home service and $15 for each month overseas. Many veterans received $1,200 to $1,800 in cash – a modestly comfortable year's income at the time. Veterans and war widows were given job preference in the civil service and at National Employment offices everywhere. The Veterans' Land Act helped to settle men on farms or small holdings of their own, or to establish them in fishing. Re-establishment credits could be used as a down payment on a house, to buy furniture or appliances, to start a small business, or to go back to school.

THE EVENING TELEGRAM

HOME EDITION

TORONTO, MONDAY, MAY 7, 1945 · 30 PAGES · PRICE THREE CENTS

WAR OVER! PEACE AT LAST

TOTAL SURRENDER SIGNED

Word Flashed At 9.36 a.m.

Gala Fete Sweeps Toronto

The Albertan

CALGARY, ALBERTA, TUESDAY, MAY 8, 1945 · 56 Pages

OFFICIAL V-E DAY TUESDAY, MAY 8

'Now We Can Really Get Started' Say Pacific Troops

FOE FIGHT ON IN CZECHOSLOVAKIA

Surrender Is Signed

Growth and Decline of Hitler Germany

Tokyo

The Weather

The Vancouver News-Herald

Metropolitan Edition

VANCOUVER, B.C., WEDNESDAY, AUGUST 15, 1945

WAR ENDS; TODAY IS V-J DAY

VANCOUVER GOES TO TOWN: From the heart of Chinatown through the West End, Pender St. was the centre of a large part of jubilant celebrations Tuesday night as residents crammed the paper-strewn downtown streets. Occidentals mingled with Orientals in the mob which jammed the Chinatown section to watch traditional Lion Dances and hear the beat of Chinese drums and cymbals. Left, a section of the crowd there can be seen. As soon as news of Allied victory was announced by the wail of sirens, permit-holders converged on liquor stores. Middle picture shows the queue which stood impatiently on the Pender St. sidewalk. Inter-service camoraderie, demonstrated throughout, was caught by the cameraman in the picture on the right. The jeepful of Pacific Command C.W.A.C.'s paused in their cruise along Pender and the metropolitan area to crowd in an excited Wren.

Police, Firemen Swamped As Vancouver Rejoices

Stores, Offices, Plants Close To Mark Peace

City Goes Wild, Stages Its Biggest Celebration

JAP WAR CHIEF COMMITS SUICIDE IN 'ATONEMENT'

NEW YORK, Aug. 15.—(AP)—Japanese War Minister Korechika ... has committed sui...

Full Surrender By Japs -MacArthur Taking Over

GUAM, July 15.—(AP)—Japanese aircraft are ...

Victories over Germany and Japan came as a long awaited relief. Vancouverites danced the boogie-woogie on Burrard Street. Toronto drivers tooted horns, and Calgarians shot off rockets.

"When we said we'd keep your job open, this is one firm that really meant it!"

Canada's repatriation programme for veterans included rehabilitation pay, clothing allowance, a year's free medical care, farming and land settlement grants, and free university and school tuition. All employers were required by law to reinstate "repats" in their pre-war jobs at former salaries.

On VE Day pandemonium broke loose in Halifax as troops stationed at "Slackers" (the naval base) ran amok. They broke into 200 stores, looted merchandise, hijacked a streetcar, and drank the city dry of 165,000 bottles of booze and beer.

Both men and women were given an extra $100 to buy civilian clothing. Ken Kenney of Thamesville, Ontario, a young piper with the Essex Scottish Regiment overseas, outfitted himself easily on that. He paid $38 for a suit with two pairs of pants and splurged $28 on a topcoat. He bought a pair of shoes for $9 and a hat for $6. He added two shirts, two pairs of socks, two sets of underwear, two ties, gloves, a scarf and a pair of rubbers.

There were even cash payments for medals of valour. Company Sergeant Major F.L. Dixon of the Essex Scottish from Windsor, Ontario, was the only man in the Canadian army to win the Military Medal three times. He was mixing sand in a foundry for sixty-seven cents an hour in March 1946 and the only good thing that had happened to him since the war, he said, was the $300 bonus he had just received for his outstanding bravery. A DVA survey of 4,000 veterans in Montreal the same month revealed that one in five was out of work and half of the remainder were dissatisfied with their jobs.

The law required employers to reinstate veterans in their old jobs at their former pay. But an eighteen-year-old butcher's assistant making $12 a week and a young shipping clerk earning $15 in 1939 wanted something better after five years of tank warfare or North Atlantic convoy duty. Charles Gage worked for six weeks in the piece goods department at Eaton's College Street store in Toronto while he was waiting to become an air-gunner in Bomber Command. When the RCAF called him up, Eaton's gave him a gold signet ring with the RCAF insignia outlined in blue and enamel and an ID bracelet. The firm sent him gift parcels at regular intervals overseas, as they did to all ex-employees in the services. When Eaton's offered him his job back, he graciously declined.

Months after the litter and damage of unofficial "celebrations" was cleaned up, parades of returning soldiers took over civic squares. Here the Royal 22e (Vingt-deuxième) Régiment du Canada *(the "Van Doos") marches through Quebec.*

The most valuable opportunities offered to the veterans were in education. Vocational schools were set up across the country, often in wartime service camps, to train 85,000 veterans as machinists, carpenters, electricians or masons. The gates of Canada's few universities were opened to a flood of veterans who could not have afforded to go in peacetime. RCAF navigator Tom Brandon of Regina, a prisoner of war at *Stalag VIIIB*, had been on a six-hundred-mile forced march across Germany, ahead of the advancing Russian army, when he found himself beside a fellow Canadian who was reading a booklet called "Back to Civil Life." One section caught Brandon's eye: "University Training: Provision is made under benefit No. 5 of the post-discharge Re-establishment Order for continued education . . . . "

By September Tom Brandon had enrolled at the University of Toronto and was quartered with many other veterans twenty-six miles east of the city at the makeshift Ajax Campus in a wartime shell factory. Tuition was free, and he had a living allowance of $60 a month on which he could scrape by. About 50,000 veterans swamped campuses across the country, where total enrolments had never yet exceeded 35,000. Enrolment at the University of British Columbia jumped from 2,900 undergraduates in 1944 to 7,300 in 1946. Army huts were hauled out on the back of the campus to squeeze everyone in.

In time the universities graduated 35,000 highly motivated veterans, many of them in two years. Among them were 8,000 engineers, 5,000 teachers and 3,000 doctors.

Co-eds found the veterans glamorous. Barbara Ewing was a co-ed at University of Toronto, and she recalled "a fantastic scramble for the attentions of the veterans." Few co-eds were well-

★★★★ Ray's 4 STAR SPECIALS

TENDER SPRING VEAL

LEG ROASTS Shank of, Lb.	23c
SIRLOIN ROASTS Lb.	29c
RUMP ROASTS Full of Meat. Lb.	30c
Loin Veal Cutlets Lb.	35c
STEWING VEAL Lb.	12c
VEAL SHANKS For Jellied Veal. Lb.	8c
Shoulder Veal Steaks Lb.	25c
BACON Sliced Back. ½ lb. cello. Each	17c
PICNIC PORK SHOULDERS. Lb.	19c
VEAL Minced Seasoned Patties. Lb.	19c
LEAN BEEF, Minced. Lb.	18c
LIVER, fresh sliced. Lb.	15c
BONELESS SMOKED PICNICS Half or Whole. Lb.	31c
BEEF Boneless. Corned Brisket. Mild Cured. Lb.	22c

With wartime price controls still in effect, Ray's Super Market in Vancouver advertised these prices for choice cuts of meat. Bargains? The average Canadian's income in 1945 was $1,538, so figure it out.

Post-War Promises

The 1945 general election was one of political promises and goodies. While Mackenzie King was worrying about Canada's obligations in post-war Europe (right), most Canadians were worrying about such day-to-day matters as jobs and families. Five years of war and the Depression had convinced many that the government owed them something, and even the capital-C conservatives knew it. "Social welfare" — the dread of most Tories and the calling-card of the socialist CCF — became the first item on the "menu" (see below). It was a close election, at least in the popular vote, but when Parliament reassembled, the Liberals had scooped both the Conservatives and the CCF in the recipe for victory.

THE CHIEF COOK COMES THROUGH

versed in sex education, and the idea of a birth control clinic on campus was unthinkable. Co-eds at "Vic," a United Church college, had available to them two books: *Birth, Marriage and Birth Control* (known familiarly as "BM and BC"), written by a United Church minister, and *The Power to Love*, which referred with delicate ambiguity to a man's power "to unlock a girl's treasure chest."

The co-eds regarded women veterans who joined their ranks as "very tough." Among those at Vic was Judy LaMarsh, an ex-CWAC who had served first as a draftswoman on the Halifax docks, and subsequently as an army linguist in the United States translating documents picked up on previously Japanese-occupied islands. She earned her BA in thirteen months and entered Osgoode Hall Law School.

"Baby Bonus"

Many veterans had matrimony on their minds. Some 40,000 of them had wed overseas. Many now married the girl back home or, if she had not waited, someone new. Married veterans made up for lost years and started families. An added incentive, if such were needed, was the controversial new Family Allowance Act. (Tory opposition MPs accused the Liberals of introducing the payments as a sop to French Canada and its traditionally large families). The monthly "Baby Bonus" ranged from $5 to $8 a month, depending on the age of the child. It was paid directly to the mother – the idea being that the father might spend it on booze rather than on the child.

In 1946 marriage meant church bells, or at least a religious ceremony. The influence of the churches was still paramount in many aspects of Canadian social life. City hall weddings or civil marriages of any kind were impossible everywhere but in three provinces: Manitoba, Saskatchewan and, after 1948, British Columbia. Couples contemplating mixed marriages – a term which meant a marriage between Protestant and Catholic or Christian and Jew – often had difficulty finding anyone willing to marry them.

Divorce was legally complicated and relatively infrequent. Except in Nova Scotia, where cruelty had been sufficient cause since the eighteenth century, the only grounds was proven adultery. This led to collusion and near perjury and created a new calling, the professional co-respondent – a woman who, for a fee, would provide "evidence." Quebec and Newfoundland had no provision for divorce. Residents there had to seek a Bill passed by Parliament in Ottawa for each couple. The Senate Divorce Committee, which heard all the evidence, was the best attended committee of any in the upper chamber.

For the veteran and his bride, as for all newlyweds, the biggest problem was finding a home. Through ten years of depression and six of war, few new houses had been built. There was an immediate need for 320,000 new homes.

"key money"

They were not quickly forthcoming. Apart from Montreal, there weren't many apartment buildings in any of the cities. Those that existed were rarely more than four storeys. Many young couples lived in rooming houses, or too often with their in-laws, with all the attendant pressures and irritations. Even light housekeeping rooms – with a hotplate, sink and kitchen table next door to a pokey bedroom – were hard to find. And the wartime practice of having to pay "key money," a lump sum of $100 to $200 for the key in addition to the rent, still continued for many flats and apartments. A number of Veterans' Housing tracts were started, providing small, utilitarian and unimaginative bungalows, and they were inexpensive and a lot better than nothing.

In January 1946 dissident veterans in Vancouver seized the empty, old Vancouver Hotel and "registered" 700 men, women and children in the rooms. Civic authorities did not eject them and, once they had squatted, provided supplies for them. In Ottawa a short and fiery ex-RCAF sergeant, Ted Hanratty, led a similar squatters' march to occupy a vacant seminary a mile from Parliament Hill. There were some confrontations with police, but since no alternative accommodation could be offered, the squatters were handled with kid gloves.

the pony photographer

In small Ontario towns like Belleville and Guelph, veterans were often more fortunate. For one dollar a veteran could buy an accessible lot of land at the edge of town. Services were usually minimal: dirt roads, water and hydro, but no costly sewers. On a quarter-acre lot septic tanks were fine. Paved roads, sidewalks, telephone lines and landscaping were unheard-of luxuries. A contractor would pour the foundations, put up the walls and roof in the house. The new owner would live for the first year with a sub-floor and exposed studding on all the interior walls except the main bedroom. The second year, if time and energy and money allowed, he would add the siding and finish the interior.

Most of the existing homes in Canada were still heated with coal, wood or sawdust fed by hopper to the furnace. The ashes were hauled out and sprinkled on the ice in winter. That made it easier for the breadman to make his deliveries, leaving his horse, with flanks steaming and hooves occasionally stamping, on the road outside. It was easier too for the milkman, glass bottles clanking against his metal basket, as he put bottles of whole milk with two inches of cream on top into the milk box. Even there, behind the small door and set

Although unemployment insurance took effect in 1941, war work took up much of the slack. With a million Canadians returning to look for peacetime jobs, more than one company accountant had to scratch his head and try to figure out what the scheme meant.

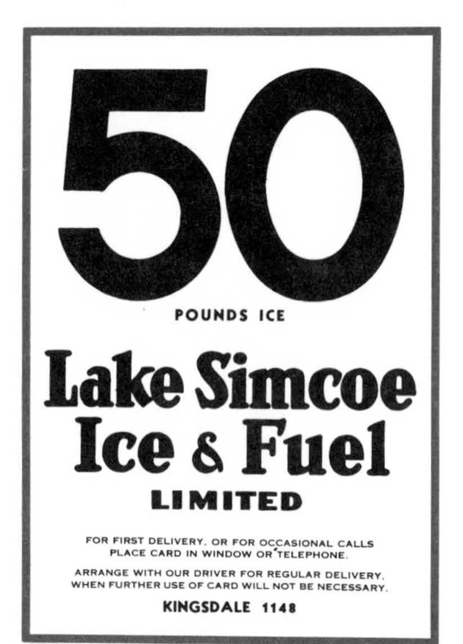

Refrigerators were hardly a new convenience for most well-to-do families, but the iceman's truck or horse still made the rounds in many neighbourhoods. This sign in the window on Wednesday or Friday brought a 50-pound block of ice for the old kitchen ice box.

into the wall, the milk still froze, pushing the cap a couple of inches into the air.

In the summer when the coal man no longer came, the ice man hefted big blocks of ice, cut the previous winter on nearby lakes or rivers, into the thousands of iceboxes still in use. Summer was the time too for the pony photographer to make his rounds, luring the kids with a pony ride and their parents with the prospect of an enlargement of Susie and Billy in the saddle.

It was also the time for the tar truck, followed by a trail of children, waiting for the moment when they could pick up a gob of tar and chew it, assuring whiter teeth. Fluoride was something you might study in Grade XII, not something mentioned in Ipana toothpaste ads. Air conditioning was a simple, inexpensive matter of either leaving doors open and screen doors shut to create a cross-draught, or closing everything to keep the heat out.

Diapers drying on the clothesline in summer smelled as fresh as new mown hay. In winter they stiffened into hard wafers and chafed the hands of housewives who unpegged and folded them. A wringer washing machine was the second or third most important appliance in most households, but despite the lure of the Easy Spin-Dry ads, few families had any sort of dryer except sunshine and fresh air.

beer parlour drinkers

The veterans themselves were chafed more often by other things – like the puritanical blue laws which banned movie shows, theatre performances, drinking in bars or organized sports on Sunday, but allowed the sports of the well-heeled such as golf, tennis, yachting and curling.

Many veterans with memories of cosy English pubs, casual Italian *trattorias*, French *estaminets* and Dutch bars grew increasingly restive at the restrictive liquor laws. In effect since the 1920s the laws had prohibited the sale of liquor by the shot and condemned beer-parlour drinkers to terms of "no standing, no games, no singing, no music"; no pictures or posters on the walls, no eating of anything except pickled eggs, no casual encounters with the opposite sex and, on the prairies, either no public drinking by women at all or separating the sexes—no men and women drinking together. On Friday nights the veterans sat around Legion halls, embroidering yarns about exploits overseas and complaining about the political power of the "drys" (the ladies of the WCTU), and the bootleggers whose business would suffer if the liquor laws were liberalized.

The Best Years of Our Lives

For all their belly-aching, however, they knew they were well off. Memories of bombed and battered Europe and its hungry, homeless people were still vivid. Some of their former comrades were less fortunate. Of a total of 53,000 wounded, 23,000 still needed hospital beds or wheelchairs or continuing treatment. The old veterans' hospitals were too crowded with the wounded of World War I to accommodate all new patients. Some were paraplegics who might never leave; others had lost legs or arms, sight or sanity. Still others were burned and disfigured or suffered neurological damage.

An American paratroop sergeant born in Sydney, Nova Scotia, spoke for all of them one night as he accepted two Oscars at the 1946 Academy Awards in Hollywood. Metal hooks now took the place of Harold Russell's hands. He won the first Oscar ever given for best supporting actor in *The Best Years of Our Lives*, a movie about veterans picking up the interrupted threads of their civilian lives. His second and special Oscar was for bringing hope and courage to his fellow veterans. He said that night: "It is not what you have lost that counts, but what you have left."

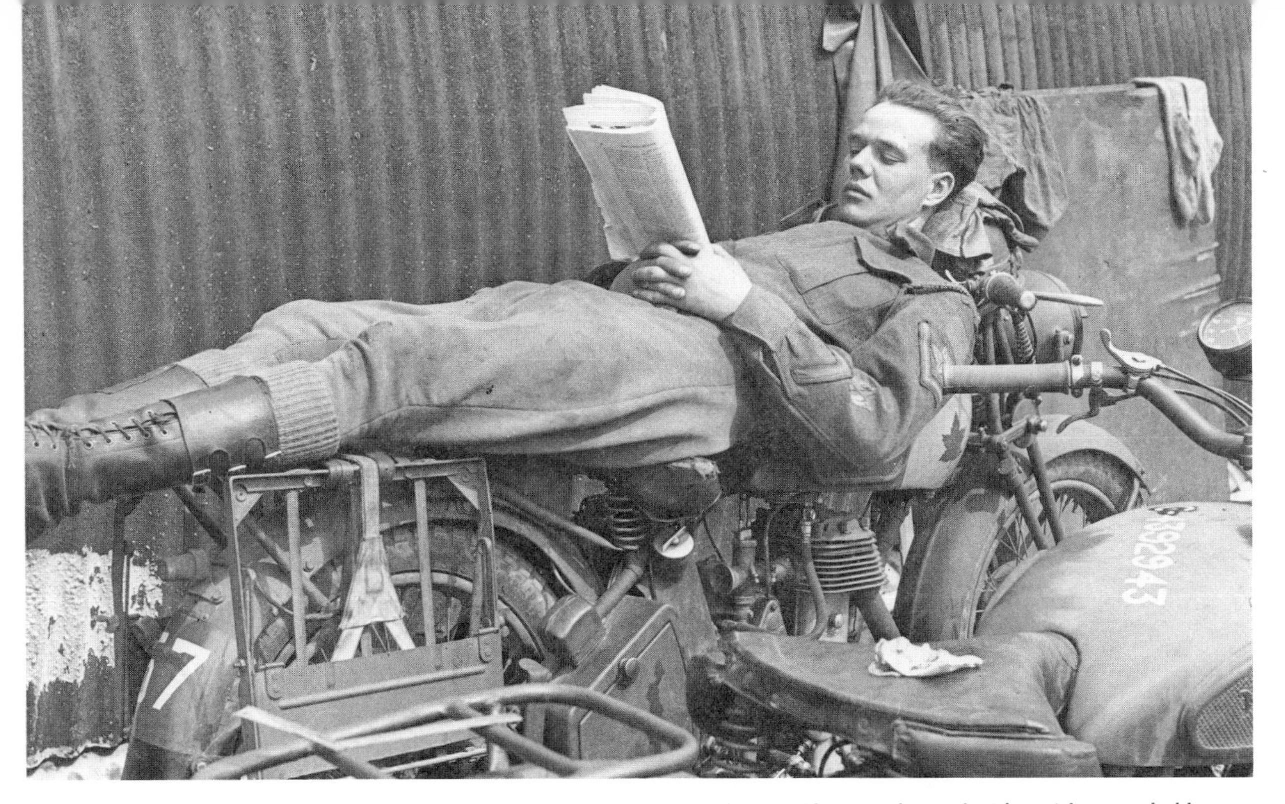

Newspapers and magazines were welcome stuffers in packages from home. Above, a dispatch rider with remarkable balance lounges on his Norton motorcycle outside the motor depot, whiling away his free time reading a medical journal.

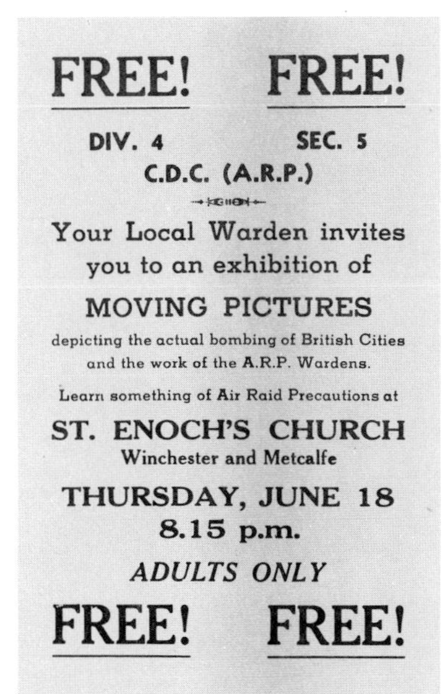

FREE! FREE!

DIV. 4 SEC. 5

C.D.C. (A.R.P.)

Your Local Warden invites you to an exhibition of

MOVING PICTURES

depicting the actual bombing of British Cities and the work of the A.R.P. Wardens.

Learn something of Air Raid Precautions at

ST. ENOCH'S CHURCH

Winchester and Metcalfe

THURSDAY, JUNE 18

8.15 p.m.

ADULTS ONLY

FREE! FREE!

No John Wayne-type commandos or Hedy Lamarr heroines in these movies at St. Enoch's Church — just a cast of Mrs. Minivers working as air-raid wardens in the rubble of bombed-out cities.

officer, Major John McDougall of Montreal. In the ensuing battles, No. 2 CFPU lost eleven men – three were killed and eight wounded.

That danger was shared by the thirty Canadian painters commissioned as Official War Artists. Charles Comfort later wrote: "One of the risks in our work was that one became deeply preoccupied and danger was upon one before it was realized." Comfort was forty-three when he left his comfortable niche at the University of Toronto to paint watercolours in a wet slit trench under enemy guns in the raw Italian winter. Carl Schaefer did many of his preliminary sketches in the cramped fuselage of a Lancaster, on bombing raids over Europe. Jack Nichols painted the hollowed faces of gun crews at action stations aboard HMCS *Iroquois*.

Molly Lamb Bobak, a twenty-three-year-old Vancouver artist was already overseas in the CWACs when she was appointed the only official woman war artist. Her light-hearted paintings of life in the Women's Corps showed another side of the war.

Meanwhile back home, another group of talented young Canadian writers, filmmakers and artists was launching a venture that was to become an important part of the Canadian cultural fabric. Some months before the war, the Canadian government had invited a top British documentary filmmaker, John Grierson, to Ottawa to advise on the production of government films. In 1939, in an old sawmill a few hundred yards from the official home of Canada's future prime ministers, the National Film Board was born.

As its first commissioner, John Grierson became a pied piper for hundreds of eager young Canadians, few of whom had any experience in film. Gudrun Bjerring, fresh from the University of Manitoba, came to interview him for the Winnipeg

Josephine Fraser of Winnipeg (seated centre) celebrated her brother's homecoming with flags, banners and a family get-together. It looks as if the furniture has been pushed aside for dancing — probably to a few scratchy 78s on the corner phonograph, or maybe to the sounds of the Fort Garry Hotel orchestra.

Leo Bachle's "famed war bird" Johnny Canuck rescues a girlfriend from a fiend.

Great Canadian Comics

Comic books became the kid-rage of the late-1930s, and before the decade's end, hundreds of thousands of copies flooded in from the U.S. every month. In December 1940, however, the government banned their importation along with all other "non-essentials," and comic book fans had to live without heroes like Superman, Flash Gordon and Captain Marvel. But not for long. Within months a shrewd Toronto promoter named Cyrus Vaughan Bell was on the market with the first Canadian comic book — *WOW*. Bell's venture made good business sense, but it took awhile before the money started coming in, and he was forced to cut back on many of the frills of *WOW*'s first issue, including full-colour printing. Buyers seemed not to mind, and kids quickly adopted the rough, tough, true-north heroes of the "whites" — Dixon of the Mounted, Dart Daring, Derek of Bras d'Or, and, of course, Johnny Canuck. The artwork for Bell's own line and the competition was first class, drawn by artists such as Adrian Dingle and Harold Town, both of whom later made their names as serious painters. Leo Bachle took the 19th century political poster character, Johnny Canuck, brought him up to date, gave him a few more muscles, and threw him into hand-to-hand combat with Japs and Germans. Not all the heroes were men: there was Nelvana of the Northern Lights, Elaine Kenyon, the Polka-Dot Pirate, and Trixie Rogers, "the famous two-fisted Wing." The heyday of the "whites" was brief, and when the U.S. border reopened, these newstand heroes vanished.

"The Invisible Commando," Lee Pierce of the RCAF, swallowed the contents of a secret capsule to make himself invisible for three hours and created havoc behind enemy lines. All comic book heroes were endowed with supernatural strength or some secret weapon. Other heroes were Thunderfist, The Brain, and Captain Wonder, all of whom donned weird costumes for their exploits.

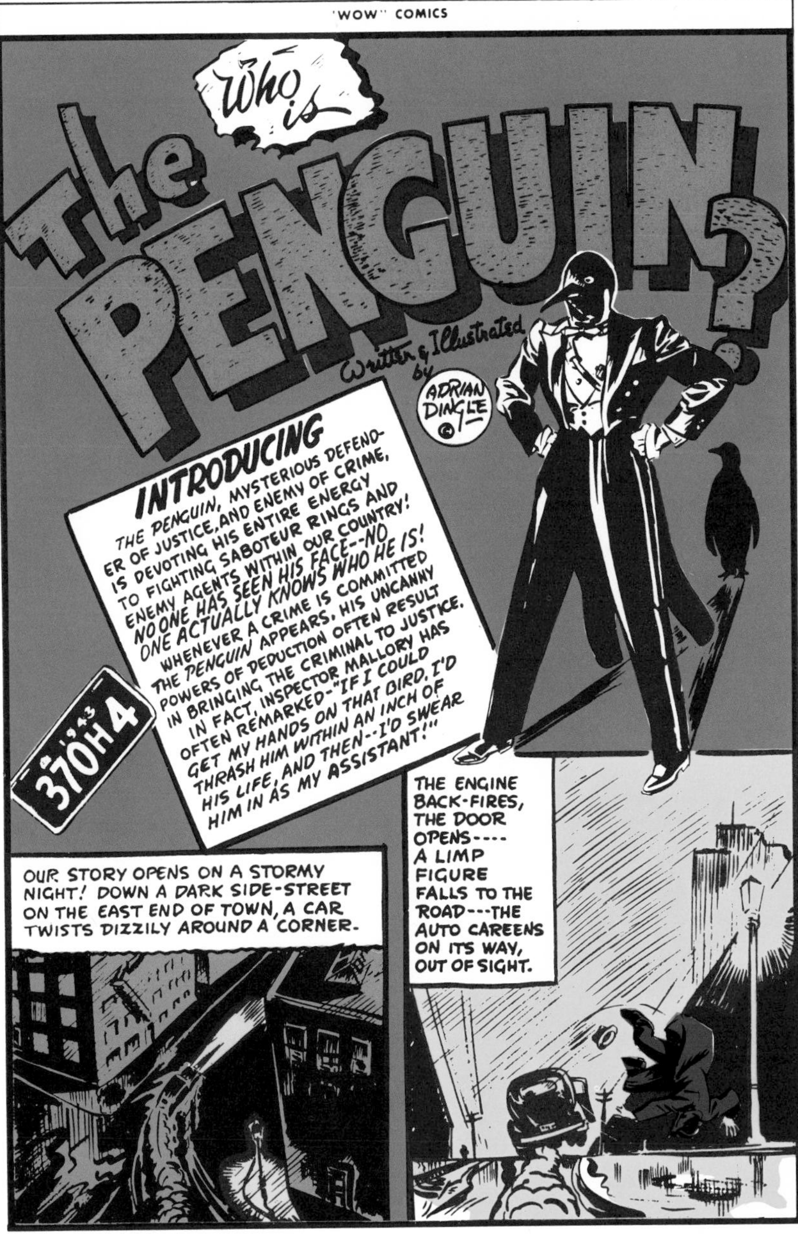

"Mysterious defender of justice and enemy of crime," Adrian Dingle's masked sleuth, The Penguin, fought underworld spy rings and saboteurs within our country. Among the other master detectives to solve their cases in the pages of Dime and Triumph comics were Nels Grant, "a hardboiled dick," Dreamer, Drummy Young, bandleader-turned-investigator, and Hugh Dunnit.

NOT WANTED
NOT WANTED
NOT WANTED
B

CHAPTER EIGHT

Displaced Persons

Question: How wide should Canada's doors be opened after the war? What restrictions would you want to see imposed? Apart from the British, what races would you welcome?

Chatelaine, January 1944

In 1945 scarcity was a way of life in Europe. Families lived in the cellars of bombed buildings; women and children grubbed for coal on the edge of railway yards. A bar of soap, a simple pad of writing paper, a box of matches or half a pound of coffee were prized possessions. Meat was often unobtainable. Medicines, particularly sulfa drugs and the new wonder drug penicillin, were in desperately short supply. Only one commodity was plentiful and that was homeless people.

Refugee camps were filled with hundreds of thousands of people culled from every war-torn country. They had been torn from their homes, separated from their families and taken to German slave labour camps. Some had fled from advancing armies. Others had survived Nazi concentration camps. Russia, with its twenty million dead and its lands laid waste by the "scorched earth" tactics of its invaders, held tenaciously to all the lands of Eastern Europe it had conquered. And thousands of refugees and Allied troops would not go home to live under its communist regime.

The United Nations called the refugees Displaced Persons; the man in the street called them "DPs." As the Canadian government cautiously opened its doors to admit an increasing flow of immigrants, DPs became the butt of many jokes and objects of derision. Nevertheless, in the peak year of 1948 no fewer than 50,000 DPs immigrated to Canada. In all more than 165,000 were admitted. The many other European immigrants who were not refugees were mostly lumped in with DPs in the popular mind.

It was a radical departure for Canada to admit *any* continental Europeans. Immigration policy had been tight and restrictive for fifteen years. While the rest of the civil service in Ottawa was expanding rapidly, the staff of the Immigration Branch, attached for some odd reason to the Department of Mines and Resources, declined thirty per cent between 1931 and 1945. Fewer immigrants were admitted in the thirties than in any decade since Confederation, and the numbers fell even lower during the war, hitting bottom in 1942 with only 7,576 arrivals, the lowest since 1860.

Canada accepted people from white Commonwealth countries, the Irish Republic and the United States: no other Europeans, no Asians, no Africans, no Latin Americans. Even in the postwar period there was no general liberalization of immigration policy. In a 1947 speech Mackenzie King affirmed: "The people of Canada do not wish, as a result of mass immigration, to make a fundamental alteration in the character of our population."

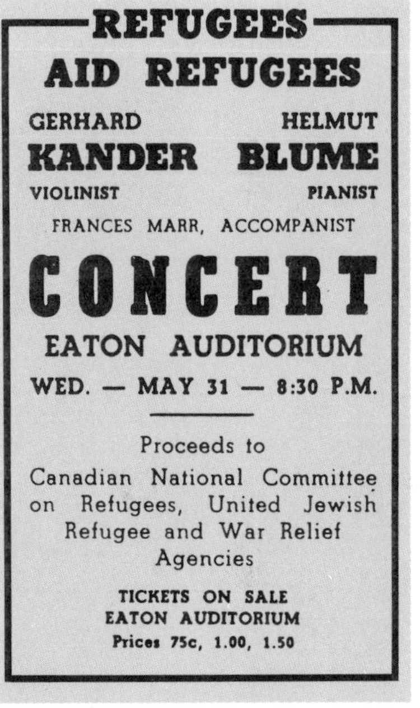

Helmut Blume and Gerhard Kander were two of the "Camp Boys" sent to Canada by British authorities in 1940 for "safekeeping." Both were German Jews who had fled the Gestapo's *reign of terror.*

Opposite page: *The first of 40,000 moms and 20,000 toddlers, the wives and children of Canadian soldiers married in England, sit among their trunks at London's Euston Station, en route to Liverpool, then Canada.*

Part of the aftermath of victory for the Allies was freeing the survivors of German POW *and concentration camps like Belsen (above). Thousands of captured Canadian soldiers and airmen suffered atrocities at the hands of* SS *goon squads, and some were murdered in retaliation for Nazi combat losses. Below, a contrast—the canteen of the* POW *camp at Sherbrooke, Quebec.*

Instead the DPS and other Europeans were admitted group by group, as special exceptions.

A small number of Europeans *had* been admitted in 1940, however. They were the unwilling and unwitting guests of the government, and they spent their first years in Canada behind barbed wire fences. They called themselves the "Camp Boys." In 1940 Britain was threatened with imminent invasion, and British authorities hurriedly made plans to ship all prisoners of war to Canada or Australia for safekeeping. As an extra precaution they rounded up all the single, able-bodied German and Austrian men under the age of thirty living in the British Isles and added them to the POW passenger manifests. Most of them were political or religious refugees from Nazi Germany. Some 2,500 civilian internees, classified as "plainly trustworthy," were thus landed at Quebec in July and August.

the Camp Boys

Canadian authorities had little warning of their arrival, and their reception was not cheery. Guards confiscated rings, watches, typewriters, suitcases and issued receipts. Then they confiscated the receipts, and none of their personal belongings were ever seen again. The guards sorted the Camp Boys out from the Nazi POWS by asking which were Jews, although a number of young priests plainly were not. In camps at Farnham and Sherbrooke, Quebec, and Fredericton, New Brunswick, they earned twenty cents a day making army kitbags and camouflage nets. For a long while there were no washrooms and not much bedding.

Gradually, a number of prominent Canadians headed by Senator Cairine Wilson sought and secured the release of the Camp Boys. Sixty per cent returned to Britain, but nearly a thousand chose to stay in Canada as "friendly aliens" and eventually as citizens. The Camp Boys were the sort of men who would oppose Hitler: young academics and intellectuals, musicians, scientists, architects, economists, left-wingers, trade union activists. Released within an average of eighteen months, they went into war plants as toolmakers or lathe operators or back to interrupted university studies.

40,000 war brides

The subsequent contributions of the Camp Boys to Canadian life were prodigious. Impresario Walter Homburger introduced Glenn Gould to the international concert world and became general manager of the National Ballet and the Toronto Symphony Orchestra. Helmut Blume, dean of the faculty of music at McGill, brought classical music and opera to radio and television. By 1944 art dealer Max Stern had established his Dominion Galleries in Montreal, and it was he who gave West Coast artist Emily Carr her first hugely successful one-woman show in eastern Canada. In Toronto, Oscar Cahen became one of the founders of Canada's postwar avant-garde art group, Painters Eleven. O.J. Feuerstein changed his name to Jack Firestone and served as chief economic adviser to Trade and Commerce Minister C.D. Howe. Firestone later donated his very substantial art collection to the nation.

The camp commandant at Sherbrooke had once told Rabbi Emil Fackenheim that, as an ex-inmate of Dachau, he should know how to stand at attention when speaking to an officer. Fackenheim later became an eminent philosopher at the University of Toronto, the same campus where Father Gregory Baum established an international reputation as a Catholic theologian. On the other hand, one of the Camp Boys who went back to England distinguished himself in other ways: physicist Klaus Fuchs became the kingpin in the international Soviet atomic spy ring.

Almost every week throughout the summer of 1944, ships crowded with women and children docked at Halifax, Nova Scotia. These women were the vanguard of over 40,000 war brides who came to Canada with their 20,000 children. One in five Canadian soldiers and airmen who went overseas a bachelor came home married.

To help prepare the war brides for their new life in Canada, Canadian military headquarters in London established the Canadian Wives' Bureau to dispense literature, give talks and show movies about the country of their destination.

Social worker Charlotte Whitton wrote a brochure entitled *From Kith to Kin*, and it was distributed to all brides overseas. It was a mixture of lyrical descriptions of the Canadian seasons and practical information of interest to women, including facts about hard water, the value of mail-order catalogues, and the perils of party-line telephones. "Two out of three farm homes have radios, one out of two has cars and about one out of three, telephones." The pamphlet introduced the women to Canadian trains: "At first sight, perhaps our 'sleepers' upset more people, unaccustomed to them, than anything else. They are perfectly safe, usually very quiet; the porter is on duty all night."

hankerings for fish and chips

The trains carried some of the war brides west to crucial first meetings with in-laws, with whom most of them would live until the war was over and their husbands came home. Heading west many were awed by the immensity of the land and its loneliness. One Scottish bride from Glasgow found herself on a quarter section of bald prairie outside Gleichen, Alberta. She wept many tears over the wood stove and the coal oil lamps, but she stayed. Army repatriation personnel followed up to see how the brides were settling in. Help came from various women's organizations like the Legionettes, the Red Cross and the YWCA.

A carton of Consuls or Exports went a long way for prisoners of war. The bribe of a pack to the right prison guard could bring temporary relief from the daily dole of bread and water. After Germany's surrender, soldiers in Europe often used smokes to buy everything from food to mementos.

All dolled-up in their Sunday best, these two English war brides catch the attention and whistles of a group of soldiers at ease outside the immigration offices in Halifax, Nova Scotia, before boarding trains for Montreal, Winnipeg and Regina. Some war brides hadn't seen their husbands since their wedding.

Many of them needed that help. Some of the Canadian boys had embroidered the truth about their life back home when they went courting. Visions of "stately homes" dissolved with the first views of clapboard Prairie houses and domestic drudgery. A few Canadian women resented the brides for snaring so many Canadian boys when they were vulnerable, lonely and far from home. Some of the homesick and disillusioned did return to the Old Country, but about ninety-five per cent overcame hankerings for fish and chips, cheery pubs and springtime in England, and settled down.

hand-picked immigrants

By May 1947 economic conditions looked bright, the expected postwar recession had not come, and there were plenty of jobs. That month, as the first group of Displaced Persons arrived in Canada, the province of Ontario launched an ambitious immigration scheme of its own. Premier George Drew, a well-to-do Tory, recognized the growing need for professional and skilled workers, but he wanted them all to be British.

The Drew Plan was the last concerted effort in Canada to restock the population with Britons. Drew took over Rainbow Corner, a large and popular wartime servicemen's club in the heart of London and mounted a major advertising campaign. Soon prospective emigrants were forming long queues outside. Berths on passenger liners were still scarce, so Drew hired a California air charter outfit to fly them to Toronto at reduced fares. At a time when few airliners carried more than a hundred passengers and the flight took seventeen hours, some 10,000 Britons reached Malton Airport that summer and early fall. Thereafter they came by sea by the thousands.

Drew's hand-picked immigrants were part of the 196,000 people who came to Canada from the United Kingdom in the forties. From Europe

Countless small adjustments were part of the education of new Canadians: "Canajun" English or French, Imperial weights and measures, dollars and cents, and a new way of life baffled many.

Military police on the docks at Bremerhaven, Germany, check the papers of this queue of refugees destined for North America. In total over 165,000 DPS were admitted to Canada.

came two other large groups, both with close wartime ties to Canada – the Poles and the Dutch.

One thousand Polish engineers and machinists had come to Canada during the war to lend their expertise to the war plants. A Polish armoured division fought as part of the 1st Canadian Army throughout the campaign in northwest Europe, and the 2nd Polish Corps was often alongside the Canadians in the long Italian campaign. Polish flyers had trained in Canada.

After the war a quarter of a million Polish refugees had the choice of returning to their Soviet-occupied country or finding another home. Late in 1946 more than 4,000 Polish soldiers, still in their army uniforms, arrived in Canada direct from Italy and Britain. Most went to work on Canadian farms under two-year contracts at $45 a month. Although they were supposed to receive the "prevailing rate," farmhands were virtually unobtainable in Canada even at $75 or $80. But no official attempts were made to enforce the contracts.

educated dishwashers

One hundred young Polish women at work in a Quebec textile mill were less fortunate. Liberal MP and wealthy millowner J. Ludger Dionne had obtained an order-in-council to bring the women to Canada. He bound them to a two-year contract and paid them twenty-five cents an hour for a normal forty-four hour week – less than half the fifty-five cents an hour paid to Quebec women. The Polish girls were also persuaded they could not marry as long as they worked there. This smacked of indentured labour, which was prohibited in Canada, and a special debate in the House of Commons was forced by CCF leader M.J. Coldwell. Opposition members had a heyday, but the debate had little result. As the Liberal government well knew, the majority of Canadians were not overly sympathetic toward DPs or open immigration policies.

Many of the Polish immigrants who came here after the war were educated people – career army officers, lawyers, engineers and other young professionals – most of whom spoke relatively good English. They took jobs as dishwashers, janitors or shippers until they could establish themselves. It was a pattern of self-help and independence generally accepted by immigrants. They worked hard, saved money, bought substantial old houses and rented rooms to pay off the mortgage.

$35-a-week domestics

There were very special bonds between Canada and Holland. Canadians had been the chief liberators of Holland. Crown Princess Juliana of the Netherlands lived in Ottawa during the war, and a room in Ottawa Civic Hospital was declared Dutch territory so that her third daughter could be born "on Dutch soil." Canada responded quickly to a request after the war to take 15,000 members of Dutch farm families from their overcrowded country of flooded farmlands and bombed cities. Canadians marvelled as Dutch families with as many as fifteen children got off trains in Vancouver or Toronto en route to nearby farmland. A further 15,000 arrived during the decade, and for years Holland expressed its gratitude with an annual gift to Canada of thousands of tulip bulbs. They would bloom each spring in the growing network of federal parkways and gardens developed in Ottawa by planner Jacques Greber.

One group of DPs owed their arrival in Canada to the enthusiasm of Brigadier C.M. "Bud" Drury, who was doing rehabilitation work in northeast Europe. In 1946 he persuaded deputy minister of external affairs Lester Pearson to tour camps set up for Baltic refugees. Their homelands in Lithuania, Latvia and Estonia had been absorbed into the Soviet Union, and as a result, many of them were admitted to Canada on condition they work for a year at menial jobs. In exclusive residential areas throughout Canada, these $35-a-week domestics were bargains for Canadian chatelaines, and more than one of the younger women proved an irresistible lure to sons of the household.

The well-organized United Jewish Relief organization in Canada brought 22,000 Jewish refugees to the country in the forties. Among them were a thousand lost or orphaned children promised homes by families in Canada. One nine-year-old boy, Jack Kuper, had roamed the Polish countryside, outwitting the Germans for years. His destination was Montreal, and when he climbed into his lower berth aboard the train from Halifax, he experienced for the first time since 1939 the incredible luxury of a bed with clean sheets, warm blankets and a soft pillow. He refused to get off in Montreal. He wanted to sleep one more night on that train, and he ended up in Toronto where he was taken into a musician's home.

abandoned children

The plight of war orphans in Greece and Italy, France and Austria was the particular concern of one dedicated and single-minded woman in Ottawa, Dr. Lotta Hitschmanova, a former Prague newspaper woman. She directed the Unitarian Service Committee of Canada, which maintained the orphaned and abandoned children in camps and homes paid for by Canadian contributions. She continued to wear a khaki uniform as a reminder that for these children the war was not yet over. A newcomer herself, Lotta Hitschmanova was a symbol, in a way, of a new Canadian concern for international peace and well-being – a concern which was to characterize both the Canadian government and people in the decades to come.

Anti-semitism reared its head in Quebec with each new influx of Jewish immigrants. For decades nationalist extremists had made Montreal's Jews the scapegoat for Québecois *business problems. For Maurice Duplessis' come-back campaign in '44* Union Nationale *posters used this caricatured Jew and his "vote of thanks" to attack Liberal premier Adélard Godbout and* PM *Mackenzie King.*

CHAPTER NINE

The Atomic Age Begins

We are at the beginning of what we think is an epoch-making period. Here is energy in a basic form never known. Where it will go is open to the imagination.

C. J. Mackenzie, president of NRC, 1945

The world's first atomic bomb exploded over the desert at Alamogordo, New Mexico, at dawn, July 16, 1945. Twenty days later a second atomic bomb, "the Little Boy," dropped from a height of six miles and exploded a fraction off target above downtown Hiroshima, Japan. The river beneath the Aioi Bridge began to boil, granite buildings within a radius of a thousand yards melted, and nearby pedestrians evaporated, leaving only a shadow imprint on the sidewalks. The explosion brought immediate death to 78,000 Japanese civilians and slower death from radiation and burns to thousands of others. After another bomb destroyed Nagasaki, the Japanese surrendered. Civilization had at last found the means to its own destruction. The Atomic Age had begun.

There is some disagreement, but some believe the uranium oxide used to develop the atomic bomb was refined in the small Ontario town of Port Hope, from pitchblende ore mined at Echo Bay on Great Bear Lake in the Northwest Territories.

French-Canadian prospector and mining man Gilbert LaBine had made the strike sixteen years earlier and opened the Eldorado Mine to extract radium. The Belgian Congo had until then held a monopoly on the radioactive element, but LaBine's new source reduced the price of radium on the world market from $75,000 to $25,000 for a single *gram*. LaBine won the covetted Curie Medal for his find. The uranium, then merely a by-product with no appreciable market value, was providently stockpiled at Port Hope. Without that uranium, the Allies could not have won the race to develop the atomic bomb.

Early in 1940, the same year the American government made an initial grant of only $6,000 for research into nuclear fission, George C. Laurence, a young physicist at the National Research Council in Ottawa, borrowed one ton of uranium-238 from LaBine and organized a small team which built a crude atomic pile. Two years later in Montreal, a joint Canadian and British team of 350 scientists and technicians were secretly at work in cramped quarters at McGill University doing research on the atomic bomb.

Thirty days after Hiroshima, Canada became the second nation in the world to possess a nuclear reactor. The Zero Energy Experimental Pile (ZEEP) "went critical" on September 5, 1945, at a secret plant 120 miles up the Ottawa River on what had a year earlier been part of Felix Beauchamp's farm. The plant was known simply as the Petawawa

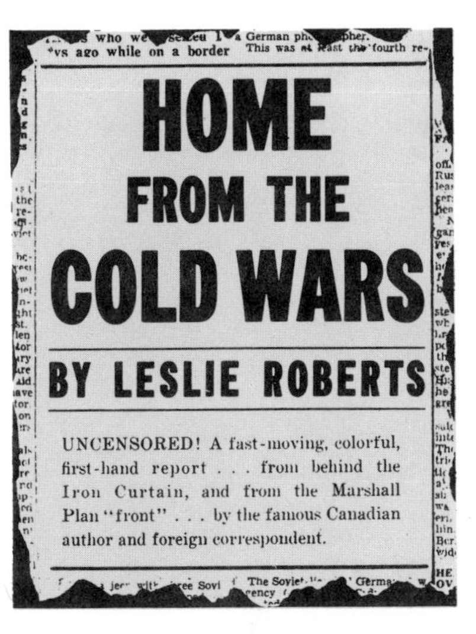

Even as the smoke of the "hot war" in Europe and Asia was clearing, new conflicts were smouldering. Allies in the war, the western nations and Russia forgot their common enemy and brought the cold war into the open. Leslie Roberts' Home From The Cold Wars *(1948) was one journalist's attempt to understand the forces of communism.*

Opposite page: *Hiroshima after the explosion of the first atomic bomb used in warfare. Two Canadian-born scientists, Walter Zinn and Louis Slotin (see page 102), had a major part in developing the weapon.*

"Tickling the dragon's tail" was Louis Slotin's term for it, and as it happened, the Winnipeg-born scientist tickled the tail once too often. Working at Los Alamos in California, he built the explosive mechanism for the world's first atomic bomb test at Alamogordo, New Mexico, on July 16, 1945. Less than a year later, while adjusting a nuclear reactor, Slotin's hand slipped and the "dragon" went wild. His quick action prevented an explosion, but Slotin himself died within days of radiation. His body was sent back to Winnipeg in a lead coffin.

Works of Defence Industries Limited. Later it became the focus of world scientific attention as the Chalk River Nuclear Laboratories.

Canada's active entry into the atomic age was an important step for a country which had only recently become highly industrialized. The only middle power to win a seat with the Big Five on the UN Atomic Energy Commission, Canada chose to concentrate on the peaceful uses of the atom – in part out of conviction and principle, but also because acquiring atomic weaponry would have been prohibitively expensive. In 1947 a second and more sophisticated reactor, the NRX, joined ZEEP. Canada's nuclear priorities were the development of nuclear power, the production of isotopes as tracers in research, medicine and industry, and the development of the Cobalt 60 Beam Therapy Unit, the first equipment of its kind for cancer treatment.

Deep River

The centre of the action was Deep River, Ontario. Scientists and their families suddenly found themselves transplanted from Montreal to this little pioneer community a few miles from the Chalk River Nuclear Laboratories. In a 1947 *Maclean's* article, Pierre Berton summed up Deep River:

No cemetery, no mothers-in-law, no traffic by-laws, no elected governing body, no slums, no main street, no private property, no taxes – and the highest birthrate in Canada.

Deep River exemplified a burgeoning Canadian belief that the present was a pathway to progress and all growth was good. It was a typical paradox that the men who had built the world's third nuclear reactor did not have paved roads in front of their homes until six years later.

On the same Wednesday in September 1945 that ZEEP went into operation, an international drama began to unfold in Ottawa. Igor Gouzenko, a young Russian cipher clerk, left the Soviet embassy after work that evening with a fistful of incriminating documents carefully hidden under his shirt. The documents proved that a massive spy ring of forty-two men and women, controlled by Soviet military attaché Colonel Nicolai Zabotin, was operating in Canada. Thirteen of its members were on the Soviet embassy staff, one was a physicist who had returned home to Britain, and the remainder were Canadians.

Gouzenko had a difficult time defecting. He went first to the Ottawa *Journal*, where night editors George Patterson and Chester Frowde missed the news scoop of a lifetime and sent him to the department of justice a block away. There an RCMP officer told him to come back in the morning. Justice Minister Louis St. Laurent was not available the next morning, and a return visit to the *Journal* produced an even more scornful rejection. That second night the city police found Anatoli Pavlov, NKVD head in Canada, and his secret police henchmen hiding in the Gouzenkos' closets. At last the defector, his family and the crucial documents were placed in the protective custody of the RCMP.

code names

Five months of undercover investigations followed, including top-level meetings with the British prime minister and the American president. The story was finally sprung by Drew Pearson, an American syndicated columnist, and the RCMP began to arrest the Canadian spies.

The spies were known only by code names, and some were never positively identified. But they included two colonels, a squadron leader, a naval officer, two scientists from the National Research Council, a member of parliament and a cipher clerk in external affairs. They had clearly penetrated the government and passed on information on the A-bomb, together with samples of enriched uranium-235. A royal commission subsequently concluded that the bulk of the technical information sought by espionage leaders related to research developments which would play an important part in the postwar defense of Canada, the United Kingdom and the United States.

Ten of the spies were convicted and received prison sentences ranging from two to six years. Nine were acquitted for lack of evidence. Among those who went to jail were Fred Rose, Labour Progressive (Communist) Party MP from Montreal, and the national organizer of the party, Sam Carr. In Britain, physicist Alan Nunn May was sentenced to ten years.

witch hunts

The Gouzenko spy trials, which ended in 1948, produced an outbreak of anti-Russian feeling in Canada that was second only in virulence to McCarthyism in the United States. "Fellow-travellers," "pinkoes," radicals, leftists and foreigners were all under suspicion. Surreptitious witch-hunts began within two government agencies: the National Film Board and the International Service of the CBC. Some staffers were fired or forced to resign. Suspicion sullied the atmosphere of both organizations, and they were effectively emasculated. The NFB was soon banished from Ottawa to the noisiest and least attractive site in all Canada for sound studios – the outskirts of Montreal at Ville St. Laurent, on the busiest flight path to nearby Dorval International Airport, and beside the projected path of Metropolitan Boulevard, the first elevated freeway in Canada and designed as a bypass for trucks.

Canadian newspapers and radio stations either ignored these witch-hunts entirely or played them down. In this they reflected public opinion. Canadians were more preoccupied with the basic ele-

Igor Gouzenko
The Hooded Informer

On the night of September 5, 1945, when a 27-year-old Soviet intelligence agent named Igor Gouzenko decided to defect to the West, he knew he was risking his life. (A few years before, former Red Army general Alexei Krivitsky, a defector living in Montreal, had been found dead in a sleezy Atlantic City hotel.) Under his shirt he had concealed 109 classified files, the importance of which he could not have fully realized. After a night of cloak-and-dagger intrigue, he finally convinced the RCMP to offer him asylum, and was whisked away to the Gatineau Hills to be grilled by the Mounties, the FBI and spymaster William Stephenson. Only a fraction of the thousand code-names in the files were then identified, but several top agents were eventually caught. Gouzenko published his story, *This Was My Choice*, in 1948, but his identity and face remain a guarded secret.

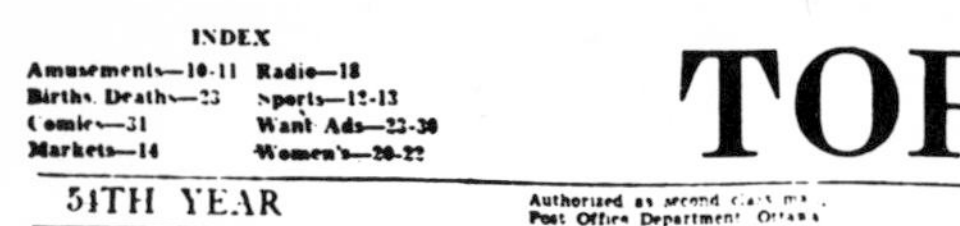

INDEX
Amusements—10-11 Radio—18
Births, Deaths—23 Sports—12-13
Comics—31 Want Ads—23-30
Markets—14 Women's—20-22

51TH YEAR

Authorized as second class mail, Post Office Department, Ottawa

TORONTO DAILY STAR

TORONTO, SATURDAY, FEBRUARY 16, 1946—34 PAGES

3c PER COPY, 18c PER WEEK

THE WEATHER
Toronto and vicinity: Milder; Sunday—Fresh northwest winds, cloudy, a little colder, snowflurries. Low tonight, 26; high tomorrow, 30.

40 TO 50 HELD IN SPY CASE RUSSIA NAMED BY MINISTER

FEDERAL CIVIL SERVANTS RESEARCH MEN ACCUSED

Royal Commission Named by Premier King to Investigate and Prosecution Will Follow Where Warranted, He Says

Ottawa, Feb. 16—An authoritative source said today detention of suspects in Canada's first major spy probe has not finished and that it is not centralized in Ottawa but spread through other parts of the country.

Information involved in the espionage activities comprised military, industrial and economic knowledge of Canada and the U.S. as a war potential, the British United Press learned

Among the many rumors—they were just that, rumors—was one which said both major and minor civil servants were involved and that at least one high-ranking government official would face serious charges.

MINISTER NAMES RUSSIA

Russia was definitely identified by a federal cabinet minister today as the unnamed country involved in an international espionage ring uncovered by R.C.M.P.

"What nation is it?" the British United Press asked him. "Obviously it is Soviet Russia," said the minister, who refused to permit his name to be used.

Members or former members of the armed forces are among those being held in connection with the espionage investigation being conducted by a royal commission, it was learned.

There was an unconfirmed but apparently accurate report that at least one member of the psychological warfare division is among those detained for questioning.

The external affairs department and the Canadian information service both denied that they knew anything about the entire division. They refused any information about the background of the man who is reported to be detained.

The office where the man worked said he has not been at work today nor was he in yesterday. They would not amplify this statement.

MAY BE 30 SUSPECTS

A government source which refused to be quoted estimated that the total of past and present Canadian government employees involved in the scandal either as suspected agents or as material witnesses, may reach a total of between 40 and 50.

Other sources declined to give the exact number because it would "not be fair." The Associated Press said 22 were held.

Some would quite possibly be released after questioning, while

HOME AND SPORT EDITION

PRIME MINISTER TOUCHES OFF SENSATIONAL INTRIGUE STORY

MOST SENSATIONAL story of espionage and intrigue since the end of war is touched off by Prime Minister King's announcement that highly confidential state secrets have bee n disclosed to a foreign power. The prime minister, shown with Hon. George Zaroubin, Soviet ambassador, and Mrs. Zaroubin, consulted Truman and Bevin before making charge

BEVIN CLASHES WITH VISHINSKY OVER LEVANT

Claims 1,700 Soviet Spies in Canada, U.S.

By DREW PEARSON
Copyright Bell Syndicate

Secret revelations are stirring in Canada. They will make people hold their hats and run for the

Instead, we've left all our cards in the hands of Joe Stalin.

There can't be any serious trouble between the British and U.S. people. We know each other. Our basic friendship is stronger than any gov-

POLISH THREAT TO YUGOSLAVIA SEEN BY RUSSIA

SPY HUNT MAY SPREAD TO WASHINGTON--REPORT

Hint Communist Organization May Be Involved—F.B.I. and R.C.M.P. Work Together in Round-Up of Accused

Ottawa, Feb. 16—(BUP)—The largest espionage ring with international ramifications far transcending the boundaries of Canada and throwing its tentacles into many districts of the United States was uncovered by the Royal Canadian Mounted Police working in closest co-operation with the F.B.I., the British United Press learned today.

Actually the Canadian arrests were made only after the U.S. government decided that the repercussions in its own country might be so far-reaching that a joint Canadian-U.S. move, once contemplated, was called off.

U.S. FEARED COMPLICATIONS

Revelation of the police roundup followed announcement by Prime Minister Mackenzie King last night that there have been "disclosures of secret and confidential information . . . to members of the staff of a foreign mission in Ottawa."

It was believed here that one of the reasons the U.S. did not take similar steps to those taken by Canada was due to the extensive ramifications of Communist organizations which might lead to a wholesale dragnet of the espionage ring being politically misconstrued, especially at this delicate stage of international discussions and acrimonious debates at the U.N.O. conference.

The Canadian arrests have been made by a sudden countrywide action simultaneously in many Canadian cities and all the material witnesses are now in custody, according to one authorized informant of the British United Press.

NO COUNTRY NAMED

The police action was completed prior to Prime Minister King's announcement. It is possible however, that the investigation now being conducted by the royal commissioners appointed and assisted by the crown prosecutor of the R.C.M.P., Gerard Fauteux, of Montreal, might necessitate further steps.

While no national has as yet been named as the power on whose behalf espionage was carried on, the British United Press learned that Communist organizations in Canada have been the "object of particular attention."

In Montreal Royal Canadian Mounted Police officers declined today to comment on an Ottawa report that four men had been rounded up in Montreal in connection with the Canadian spy probe. They said "all information must come from Ottawa."

The U.S. state department said that it had been notified 48

The headline that took five months to hit the front page is emblazoned across the February 16, 1946 edition of the Star. *Yet, on September 5, 1945, when Soviet agent Igor Gouzenko defected with details of the story, no one wanted to believe him. He first went to the Ottawa* Journal, *where editors thought the story preposterous.* PM *Mackenzie King (seen here with Soviet ambassador Zaroubin) at first wanted to hand Gouzenko and his files back to the Soviets.*

ments of postwar progress: plants and industries which would produce jobs, more houses, more civic improvements, rural electricity, and above all bridges, culverts and hard surface pavement.

Blacktop was the standard political promise at provincial elections in the forties. In southern Canadian cities it was always easy to detect visitors from northern towns by the pitted windshields of their cars. In Quebec, under the autocratic premiership of Maurice Duplessis, roads would change from blacktop to gravel at the boundaries of *Union Nationale* and Liberal ridings.

In 1912 a highway enthusiast in Victoria, A.E. Todd, had offered a gold medal for the first person to drive a motor vehicle along an all-Canadian highway route from the Atlantic to the Pacific. No one claimed it until 1946, when Brigadier R.A. Macfarlane and Kenneth MacGillivray drove the 4,743 miles from Louisbourg to Victoria in their 1946 Chevrolet in nine days. Previous contestants had been forced to load their automobiles on to railroad flatcars for some of the way, or put on flanged wheels and ride the tracks themselves.

a two thousand mile detour

The highway across northern Ontario from Nipigon to Geraldton did not exist until the middle of the decade, and a two-thousand-mile detour through the United States was necessary to drive the 150 miles between the two towns. In British Columbia there was no road through the mountains from Golden to Revelstoke until 1940, when the Big Bend highway, open only in summer, cut a 190-mile gravel loop along the Columbia River. Even then only the most intrepid drivers braved it. Most Canadians driving west to Winnipeg went via Michigan, Illinois and Wisconsin; travellers coming from the West drove through Montana, Idaho and Washington. In 1949 the Trans-Canada Highway Act provided funds for a highway, but it would be thirteen years before it was finished.

The epic road construction job of the decade was the building of the Alcan Military Highway from Mile Zero at Dawson Creek, British Columbia, to Fairbanks, Alaska, 1,523 miles away. Seventeen thousand Canadian and American construction workers and ten thousand American troops worked day and night, seven days a week, to build the highway in eight months. In November 1942 it opened for traffic, and a year later it had been graded and improved as a good all-weather gravel highway. All but 302 miles were in Canada, and it helped open up both the Peace River country and the Yukon Territory.

a "two-elevator town"

Although Dawson Creek is in British Columbia, it was only accessible by road from Alberta. Alberta benefited from all the construction activity, but by the end of 1946 the wartime activity had ceased. More and more young Albertans left the farms in search of jobs back East, and the population of the province began to decline. On the horizon loomed the spectre of diesel instead of steam locomotives on the two transcontinental railroads, and that spelled disaster for Alberta's coal mines. That year Canada imported sixty-three of the seventy-one million barrels of crude oil it needed, and the domestic source in the Turner Valley oilfield southwest of Calgary was running out at a rate of ten per cent each year.

So, prospects for Alberta were not auspicious on November 20, 1946, when Vern "Dry-Hole" Hunter, a thirty-nine-year-old tool-push for Imperial Oil, moved a drilling rig onto Mike Turta's 160-acre farm west of Leduc. Imperial's drilling record had been disappointing: 133 dry holes and not one producing well. But by the beginning of February 1947, Hunter and his crew had the drill bits down to 5,066 feet.

Fred Rose
The Spy in the House

One of the twelve Canadians netted in the RCMP's round-up of Soviet sympathizers and spies was MP Fred Rose (Rosenberg). On February 15, when he was arrested on charges of espionage, he blurted, "But, honest to God, I'm innocent," but his plea was ignored. His association with the Communist Party since 1927 and the files of Russian defector Igor Gouzenko suggested the contrary. He was a Polish Jew by birth, a Canadian citizen since 1926, and in 1943 had been elected to the Commons as Labour Progressive MP for the working-class riding of Montreal-Cartier. At odds with the federal government over the War Measures Act, and the Québecois over his pamphlet, *Hitler's Fifth Column in Quebec,* he was linked with recruiting Soviet spies and sentenced to six years in jail.

The corner post office in Leduc, Alberta, was still the busiest place in town in 1948, but the talk of the town was oil. From the day that Vern "Dry Hole" Hunter spudded-in Imperial Oil's first well, on February 13, 1947, over 150 new rigs had cropped up on the horizon on the outskirts of the town.

The fewer than a thousand people of Leduc, a "two-elevator town" eighteen miles south of Edmonton, were not impressed. "Most of us wouldn't have known an oil well if it came out and bit us," said Fred Johns, editor of the weekly Leduc *Representative*. But Imperial Oil was confident enough to invite the press and a party of official guests out from Edmonton on Thursday, February 13, to watch Dry-Hole Hunter bring in a producing well. They were joined by the curious and the uninvited who stood around on the snow-covered wheat field in the routine fourteen-below (F.) weather, fortified by coffee, sandwiches, pickles, cake and donuts hurried in from the Cottage Tea Room in Edmonton. At four in the afternoon they heard the cry: "Here she comes. It's oil."

twenty large smoke rings

Roughneck Johnny Funk lit some sacks tied to the end of a rope, whirled them around his head and heaved them into the sump pit. Flames whooshed fifty feet into the air. The discovery well belched up spasmodic bursts of oil, water and flaming gas. Twenty large smoke rings formed in the crisp blue sky signalling a new era of prosperity for Alberta and for Canada. Farmer Mike Turta became prosperous overnight, but not wealthy like the oil millionaires of Oklahoma and Texas. Like most Alberta farmers, he did not own the mineral rights to his land. They were retained by the provincial government, and Social Credit Premier Ernest Manning wisely husbanded Alberta's new wealth from oil royalties.

Some of the money Canadians earned was spent in the United States, even though the Canadian dollar bought only ninety cents in U.S. currency. To keep Canadian dollars at home travellers were legally limited to spending $25 on trips south of the border. This at a time when "class" for most Canadians was to be found in the United States: they could see live major league baseball, drink whisky by the shot in real bars, order a crisp salad any season in a restaurant, and stay in one of the new motels which were beginning to replace the little cabins of tourist camps and auto courts.

There was also the lure of American clothing (always six months ahead of Canadian fashions), American cottons, American appliances and American cigarettes. Lucky Strikes or Camels sold for around twenty-three cents a pack, fifteen cents cheaper than cigarettes in Canada, and they were smuggled by the truckload across the Quebec border. The alternative for many Canadians on modest salaries was "roll-your-owns" made singly by hand or with a V-Master machine.

For the working stiff who often preferred "makin's" to "tailor-made" cigarettes, the work week was long and the pay envelope pretty thin. When the decade began there were only 360,000 trade union members in Canada, and although that number doubled during the war there were still basic divisions between the old Trades and Labour Congress, affiliated with the American Federation of Labor, and the Canadian Congress of Labour. In Quebec there were further divisions with the Catholic unions.

illegal strike

But labour was determined to flex its muscles after the war. Loggers in British Columbia, auto workers at Ford in Windsor, Ontario, packing house operatives across the country, all went out in unprecedented numbers to back up their demands for higher wages, shorter hours and union recognition. Some strikes were violent, others drawn-out: a printers' strike against newspapers in the Southam chain lasted for forty-one months! Most walkouts were at least partly successful. The years 1946 and 1947 set new records for strikes and work hours lost, but the most spectacular

The return of the veterans sparked a dramatic increase in the number of marriages — 33,000 more in 1946 than there had been in 1944. Wartime shortages, however, were still commonplace, especially in housing, and many newly-weds were forced to put up with in-laws before moving into flats and houses of their own.

Georges-Henri Lévesque
Apostle of a New Order

When the Massey Commission on the national development of the arts, letters and sciences was formed in 1949, Pére Georges-Henri Lévesque was named its vice-chairman. As the director of Laval University's new *Faculté des Sciences Sociales,* he had already made waves for Quebec premier Maurice Duplessis, when he joined liberal prelates of the Church in backing striking miners at Asbestos. (The strike leader was Jean Marchand, a former student of Lévesque's.) When the Massey Commission tabled its report, one of its key recommendations was more federal funding to universities and colleges, but before the programme could be effected at Laval, premier Duplessis branded the university a hotbed of communism and socialism, and Lévesque was forced to resign. He was offered a seat in the Senate but turned it down in favour of the president's post at the University of Rwanda in East Africa in 1963.

strike of the decade came near its end.

On November 28, 1948, over two thousand workers at the Johns-Manville plant in Asbestos, Quebec – the largest asbestos plant in the world – went on strike. They wanted a fifteen-cent-an-hour wage increase, to bring them to a dollar an hour, and a clean-up of the hazardous dust-filled plant. Quebec Premier Maurice Duplessis, who also acted as the province's attorney-general, sent 150 Quebec Provincial Police into the town to maintain law and order. Their behaviour was so drunken and provocative that the municipal council successfully requested their recall. The strikers were joined by 2,500 other asbestos workers from nearby Thetford Mines, and the illegal strike continued through March and April.

Dictatorial, ultra-conservative and a narrow Quebec nationalist, Duplessis ruled the province with the support of the powerful English-Canadian business establishment and the conservative elements of the Roman Catholic hierarchy. Duplessis was anti-labour, as he said in 1948: "Labour has the right to organize, but not to disorganize." But the situation at Asbestos was rather more complex: the striking workers were all affiliated with the Canadian Confederation of Catholic Workers, of which the secretary-general was Jean Marchand.

400 QPP arrive

On May 4, at a mass meeting at Thetford Mines, the strikers learned that the American Johns-Manville company planned to bring in scab workers escorted by the Quebec Provincial Police. On May 5 the strikers seized the town of Asbestos, set up barricades and roadblocks on the five roads into town, and captured twelve Quebec provincial policemen. They roughed them up, handcuffed them and briefly held them prisoner in the basement of St. Aimé parish church, the strikers' headquarters. The strikers then attended midnight mass and most went home to their families.

A force of four hundred Quebec Provincial Police, armed with machine guns, tear gas and riot control weapons, arrived during the night, broached the barricades, dragged forty strikers from the sanctuary of St. Aimé's and beat them unmercifully in a display described by *Time* magazine as "sickening." One hundred and eighty battered strikers in all were arrested and taken to jail in Sherbrooke.

a vehement May Day sermon

The Asbestos strike anticipated a revolution, one which would sweep through Quebec a decade later. Ranged against Duplessis were several men who would make names for themselves. One was Father Georges-Henri Lévesque, founder and dean of the school of social studies at Laval University. Jean Marchand led the strikers, and Jean Drapeau, a crusading young lawyer, defended them. Gérard Pelletier, who had earlier researched industrial disease in the asbestos mines for the Jesuit publication *Relations*, reported on the situation for *Le Devoir*, and Pierre Trudeau, who had been present during part of the 142-day strike, later edited a book of essays and articles about it. Archbishop Joseph Charbonneau preached a vehement May Day sermon in support of the strikers.

The consequences for Charbonneau were grim. A venomous Duplessis determined to rid himself of the archbishop and used secret funds from his *caisse électorale* to pay for complicated intrigues at the Vatican. Shortly afterward the Archbishop resigned for reasons of ill health, and plain Father Joseph Charbonneau, in a threadbare soutane with $70 in his pocket, took the train west, pausing just long enough to observe that he was in radiant good health. He became a hospital chaplain in Victoria, B.C.

Quebec premier Maurice Duplessis (with scissors), Montreal archbishop Joseph Charbonneau, and a member of the QPP *(wearing "shades") are surrounded by politicians, police and public for the 1946 opening of the Ste.-Thérèse Bridge. Three years later,* le Chef *banished Charbonneau for backing Asbestos strikers.*

1940: *Wheat farmers harvest record ½ billion bushels.*

1942: *Alcan Highway opens – built in nine months.*

1944: *30,000 Canadians join in D-Day invasion of Normandy.*

1947: *Oil discovery at Leduc ushers in new age of prosperity for Alberta.*

All Canada cheered when Barbara Ann Scott returned to Ottawa in 1947 with the world figure skating title, and generous fans showered her with presents. When sour-puss Olympic committee officials objected, she handed back the keys to the new convertible, kept her amateur status, and swept the Olympics in 1948.

CHAPTER TEN

Canada's New Look

Yet this upstart cock o' the north is more compass than weather vane . . . pointing all along to a goal that greater nations have missed by going off in opposite directions, usually in a huff.

Gerald Anglin, *Canada Unlimited* (1948)

"Just like a fairy princess"–pretty, with blonde hair, sparkling blue eyes, a soft sweet voice and a winsome smile. Clearly a nice girl, polite and respectful to her elders. Ottawa women remembered how, as a child, she had performed in the annual show at the exclusive Minto Skating Club. Barbara Ann Scott was the perfect heroine for the forties.

She was a superb and highly competitive figure skater, the first woman to win the Lou Marsh Trophy as outstanding Canadian athlete of the year. She was still only eighteen the following year, 1947, when she won the European ladies' figure skating championship in Switzerland and capped her triumph by taking the world championship in Stockholm a few weeks later.

There were 70,000 fans on hand to welcome her home to Ottawa when her train steamed into the station. The city gave her a cream-coloured Buick roadster. Her shirred beaver coat with the puffed sleeves was fashion-famous. And the aging prime minister, Mackenzie King, a glint in his eye, kissed her and laughed with her when she had difficulty wielding the champagne bottle to christen the *Miss Barby* at the CNE.

To all fairy princesses, eventually an ogre appears, and Barbara Ann's was Avery Brundage, crusty president of the U.S. Olympic Committee, who pointed out that if she kept the car she would lose her amateur status for the upcoming Olympics at St. Moritz. Canadians exploded with public outrage at this intrusion into dreamland, and the matter was raised in the House of Commons. But Barbara Ann Scott bowed to the inevitable and handed back the car keys, and went to Europe to win the Olympic gold medal.

With no more amateur worlds to conquer, she turned professional, and this time she happily accepted a powder blue convertible. She was paid $80,000 for an eight-week run at the Roxy Theatre in New York, then starred in a number of American ice shows.

While thousands of Canadian girls took up figure skating in the wake of Barbara Ann Scott's success, their mothers and older sisters concerned themselves more with being feminine than with being competitive. An obscure young Paris couturier, Christian Dior, had just introduced the "New Look." Within months inexpensive copies were run up by dress manufacturers in New York, Montreal and Toronto, and the majority of women between fourteen and forty happily traded the austere, military look of squared shoulders and straight skirts for swirls of materials to accentuate

Canada's entry into the field of magazine photo-journalism in the forties was New World. *However, its attempt to compete with its thicker, glossier, American competitor,* Life, *was a dismal failure, and the magazine folded before the end of the decade.*

Margaret Marshall — Miss Canada 1947 — seems to be enjoying the fuss and the flashbulbs on this Montreal stage. After years of wearing overalls in wartime factories, it was time to be "pretty."

hips, bustlines and tiny waists.

Skirts billowed out and down to within twelve inches of the ground. Tycoon-turned-movie-producer Howard Hughes engineered the cantilever brassiere for Jane Russell, buxom young star of *The Outlaw*. That set the trend for what came to be known as "uplift." Further refinements produced the strapless bra and the strapless formal gown.

shorts in a public place

By the summer of 1948 women were cautiously adopting some new warm weather items. From the French Riviera came the bikini, named after the tiny atoll in the South Pacific where the United States was testing the A-bomb. But the bikini wasn't to be seen on public beaches from Vancouver's English Bay to the sand dunes of Prince Edward Island. Most young women who dared took to sunning themselves on what was now called the patio. In Montreal there was a fine of $15 for any woman caught wearing shorts in a public place, whether pushing a stroller around the block or sunning herself in a neighbourhood park. In Ottawa press photographer Marge Shackleton scandalized the capital city when she wore slacks on the job.

To most women the matter of shorts, slacks and bikinis was a frivolous issue. They had more important things to worry about. Nineteen years after women had won the right to vote, there was not one woman MP in the House of Commons. Many who had satisfactorily filled jobs vacated by men during the war years were forced to return to the kitchen sink or the secretary's desk.

The New Look came to symbolize a new order. It was a world in which William Lyon Mackenzie King, a lonely old bachelor of seventy-four felt increasingly uncomfortable and weary. Early in 1948 he asked the Liberal Party to call a leadership convention – the first since 1919, when King himself had been chosen successor to his political idol, Sir Wilfrid Laurier. In August the Liberals elected Louis St. Laurent their new leader on the first ballot. But power long held was hard to give up, and it was not until he became ill in England in November that King relinquished the prime ministership.

Mackenzie King had been prime minister longer than any man in the history of the British Commonwealth. He had outlasted Churchill. He had outlived Roosevelt. He had been prime minister for all but five years and a few months since 1921, and for almost two decades Canada had been led by bachelors, King and R.B. Bennett.

In public life Mackenzie King had been an economist, a labour conciliator, a civil service mandarin, and an adroit political leader. In private he lived in Laurier House with ghosts of the past, alone with his dog, communing with his mother (dead since 1917), accepting the Order of Merit from King George VI only to hang it on the wall beside the WANTED poster of his rebel grandfather, William Lyon Mackenzie. At Kingsmere, his summer home in the Gatineau Hills, he sat in the twilight among his "ruins," the fragments of historic buildings which he had erected in a sort of Druidic circle on the lawns. He consorted with mediums and spiritualists. When he retired, a long era in Canadian politics came to an end.

supporter of international peace

Louis St. Laurent was a prominent lawyer from Quebec City who had come to Ottawa and entered politics only out of a wartime sense of duty. St. Laurent ran the government in the manner of a successful and self-assured chairman of the board of a corporation.

For his new minister of external affairs, St. Laurent chose a professional diplomat, Lester Pearson. Hitherto Canada had been more concerned with its own problems than those of the world. But now, as an industrial nation unscarred by war and untainted by imperialism, a new international role emerged. Canada became a staunch and enthusiastic supporter of international peace through the United Nations and all its agencies.

The most outstanding example of Canada's new-found international spirit was Dr. Brock Chisholm, the only psychiatrist ever to head the medical services of a nation's army. An expert administrator with a legendary scorn for red tape, Chisholm became the first director general of the UN's World Health Organization in Geneva. His best known maxim was: "You can only cure retail, but you can prevent wholesale." Chisholm defined health as "a state of complete physical, mental and social well-being and not merely the absence of disease and infirmity," and that definition became the cornerstone of the WHO.

unfinished business

International medical teams worked successfully to combat glaucoma in Africa and a rare tropical disease in Indonesia. They defeated epidemics in the Middle East and established a world-wide epidemic warning system. Chisholm was one of the first to predict the population explosion on the distant horizon and the full horrors of nuclear war.

Domestically, however, there was still one piece of unfinished business on Canada's postwar agenda: the fate of the oldest colony in the British Empire, Newfoundland. The island had lost its Dominion status in 1934 when it went belly-up financially, and ever since it had been in political receivership, governed by an appointed commission rather than an elected assembly. The war brought modest prosperity to Newfoundland. Thousands of Canadian and American troops were stationed there, and activity at Gander air-

The federal government's plan for post-war economic reconstruction dominated the Dominion-Provincial Conference of August 1945, and the big question facing PM King was, would the provinces "jump or bite."

Remember When....

. . . the ice man, the milk man and the coal man came around? Shopping at the grocer's, the butcher's, the bakery, the fish store? Father would put in the clutch and coast down hills on the Sunday drive. And near the U.S. border, older kids would huddle around the radio at night and listen to "The Shadow," "Inner Sanctum," "Gang Busters" and "The Green Hornet" — scared half out of their wits. You didn't take a date to a bar, you took her to the soda fountain. Frank Sinatra was the "king of the crooners" – American, of course. Mondays were washdays . . . the old wringer washer. And dishes? Everyone helped out . . . once in awhile. Going on a trip? You took the train somewhere. And remember when . . .

Two English war brides perch on chrome and vinyl stools in this Montreal soda fountain, as the "jerk" behind the counter serves up ice cream sodas.

The corner of Ontario and Downie in Stratford, Ontario, is typical turn-of-the-decade small-town Canada: no traffic lights yet, but a few late model Meteors.

Prime Minister Mackenzie King and Joey Smallwood of Newfoundland sit side by side at the National Liberal Leadership Convention in August 1948 — both, in a sense, "between jobs." King had announced his resignation in January, but was to hang on to the PM*'s office until November (establishing a Commonwealth record of 7,825 days in office). Smallwood had shepherded the island's pro-Confederation forces to victory in the referendum of July, but would have to wait eight months before taking office as the first premier of Canada's tenth province.*

port and at the port of St. John's had increased dramatically.

In 1946 a National Convention of forty-five members was elected to chart the future of Newfoundland. The Convention held a referendum, on which Newfoundlanders were given three options. The first was to continue as a British colony, ruled by a governor and civil service bookkeepers anxious to retire the island's debts. The second was to return to self-government. The third was to enter the Canadian Confederation.

When the same question had come up in the 1860s, Newfoundland's anti-Confederation forces had won. Their slogan had been: "Come near at your peril, you Canadian wolf." The traditional mistrust of all islanders for all mainlanders hadn't changed much in the years between. During the war many Newfoundlanders preferred the friendly, open-handed Yanks to Canadians stationed at the naval base at Argentia, the air force base at Stephenville, and the army base at Fort Pepperell. And there were moves toward joining the United States. London and Ottawa would have none of it. They did not want to see Canada sandwiched between Alaska and an offshore American domain in Newfoundland.

delegations to Ottawa

Nevertheless, a movement for economic union with the United States did get off the ground, led by a young radio station owner, Geoff Sterling, and his on-air star, Don Jamieson.

Newfoundland sent delegations to Ottawa and London to determine which would offer the best deal. Britain was financially drained by the war, and the Labour government was already dismantling the Empire. Britain offered a return to self-government and independence, but the Liberals in Ottawa offered the more tangible benefits of expanding social welfare: unemployment insurance, family allowances and the same deal for Newfoundland that was enjoyed by Canadians.

Emerging as the leader of the pro-Confederation camp was a newspaperman and sometime farmer named Joey Smallwood. He had written and edited a best-seller entitled *The Book of Newfoundland*, which he transcribed into a popular radio program. He fought his campaign on radio, in the newspaper, and with numerous visits to isolated outports.

a "kicker"

The results of the referendum in June 1948 were inconclusive. The votes tallied 69,000 for self-government, 64,000 for union with Canada and 22,000 for no change in the island's status. In a second vote a month later, with only two alternatives on the ballot, union with Canada won over independence by a margin of 7,000 votes.

On December 11, 1948, Louis St. Laurent declared: "We the people of Canada look forward to the last great step of Confederation," and signed the Terms of Union with Newfoundland. Even then there was a "kicker," as Joey Smallwood, the first premier of the province belatedly discovered. Some tidy mainlander in Ottawa had set the date of entry to coincide with the start of a new fiscal year on April 1, 1949, forgetting that this was April Fool's Day. Smallwood would have none of that. The entry of the tenth province was pushed ahead to 11:55 P.M., March 31.

Canada now stretched from Ucluelet on Vancouver Island clear across to the other side of the continent and 500 nautical miles eastward into the North Atlantic. Also, largely unnoticed in the turmoil of war, Sergeant Henry Larsen and the crew of the RCMP schooner *St. Roch* had sailed through the Northwest Passage in both directions, reinforcing Canada's unsubstantiated claims to the islands of the Arctic archipelago.

If Canada seemed geographically complete, in other areas there were enormous gaps. The literature of the forties was small in volume: in no year did Canadian book publishers together issue as many as one hundred books. There were few soldier poets this war, and apart from E.J. Pratt's epic poems, *Dunkirk* and *Behind the Log*, the war was largely ignored. Earle Birney's novel about the comic misadventures of Private Turvey, Ralph Allen's *Home Made Banners*, a straightforward drama of a foot soldier in action, and Hugh Garner's *Storm Below*, a novel about messdeck life aboard a corvette, were among the few fictional efforts to emerge from six years of battle. The one major stage star to emerge did so in *Tit-Coq*, a play about a jaunty French-Canadian soldier: Gratien Gélinas wrote, directed and starred in the comic hit of the decade.

Two Solitudes

In a country without so much as a National Library, it was difficult for an author to make a living from books, whether fiction or non-fiction. Mazo de la Roche was one of the few writers to earn a substantial income from her books. She continued her sequence of historical novels about "Jalna" and the saga of the Whiteoak family, publishing five new books in the forties.

At the same time a new generation of novelists was emerging, whose works were to engage Canadians for decades to come. Foremost among them was a former St. Boniface, Manitoba, schoolteacher, Gabrielle Roy, whose *Bonheur d'occasion* (*The Tin Flute*) revealed the life of French-Canadians in the Montreal slums. The novel won the Governor General's Award in 1947 and the prestigious *Prix Fémina* in France.

Gwethalyn Graham's Montreal love story, *Earth and High Heaven*, dealt with the provocative and hitherto taboo subject of anti-Semitism. In

Hugh MacLennan
Novelist Rising

Somewhat obscured by the war, the forties saw the emergence of many new writers in English and French Canada, among them novelist Hugh MacLennan. Born in Glace Bay and raised in Halifax, Nova Scotia, his first novel, *Barometer Rising* (1941), was set against the backdrop of Halifax in 1917, ending with the explosion that devastated the city. Living in Montreal from 1935, he set his second book, *Two Solitudes* (1945) in Quebec, unfolding in its story the age-old conflicts between the province's two cultures. The novel was at once a success, and before the end of the decade, a third book titled *The Precipice* (1948) earned him a reputation as one of the finest English writers of Canadian fiction.

- JIVE LANGUAGE -

Boogie-Woogie	Heavy Bass Harmony
Bust Your Conk	Apply Yourself Diligently, Break Your Back
Bree	A Girl
Buddy Ghee	A Fellow
Dicty	High Class
Dillinger	A Killer-Diller
Fruiting	Feeling Around
Free By	No Charge, Gratis
Gobstick	Clarinet
Hepcat	Guy Who Knows
Hincty	Conceited or Snooty
Home-cooking	Very Fine
Icky	One Who is not Hep
In the Groove, Down the Alley	Perfect
Jive	Lingo or Speech
Jitter Bug	Swing Fan
Jitter Sauce	Liquor
Kopasetic	Absolutely Okey
Knock Me	To Obtain
Latch on Grab	Get Wise To
Lilly Whites	Bed Sheets
Lip Horn	Saxophone
Long Hair	Prefers the Classics
Lay-Your-Racket	To Jive, Sell an Idea
Lane	A Male
Licks	Hot Musical Phrases
Muggin	Making 'Em Laugh
Mouse	Pocket
Mess	Good
Man on the Hitch	Man on the Make
Neigho-Pops	Nothing Doing, Man
Ofay	White Person
Off the Cob	Corny
Out of this World	Perfect Rendition
Rock Me	Send Me
Rug-Cutter	Very Good Dancer
Togged to the Bricks	Dressed to Kill
Truck on Down	To Go Somewhere
Trickeration	Strut Your Stuff
Twister to the Slammer	Key to the Door
Trilly	To Leave, Depart
Un Hipped	Not Wise to the Jive
V-S	Chick Who Spurns Company
Whipped Up	Beat, Exhausted
What's Cooking	A Swell Picture

Brassy big-band jazz had an effect on street-talk as well as music in the forties. This "Jitterbug's Jive Dictionary" was part of the promo for the Toronto premiere of What's Cookin', *a jazz hit with Woody Herman and the "swing-sational" Andrews Sisters.* (Out of this world.)

Vancouver Ethel Wilson's first novel, *Hetty Dorval*, won international acclaim as a novel about a woman incapable of affection. In 1945 Hugh MacLennan, a classics teacher at Montreal's Lower Canada College, wrote a novel probing the generations-old gulf between French and English Canada, and its title, *Two Solitudes*, later became the political catch-phrase for the entire country.

"Command Performance"

When the boys came home from overseas, radio returned to centre-stage in popular entertainment. Comedy, music, drama, children's programmes and public affairs forums took the place of wartime news and views broadcasts. Canadians living near the U.S. border could, of course, pick up their daily dose of American situation comedies, soap operas, live big-band broadcasts and cops-and-robbers shows, but the CBC and local stations were slowly learning how to woo listeners to their own frequencies.

"Command Performance" and "Borden's Canadian Cavalcade" paid a well-deserved musical and dramatic tribute to Canada's war heroes. "New Canadians" introduced the country to displaced persons who were arriving daily from Europe. There were "soaps" like "John and Judy"; family dramas like "The Jacksons" in Winnipeg, "The Gillans" in the Maritimes, "The Carsons" in B.C.; and public opinion shows like "What's Your Beef" and "Citizen's Forum." Thousands of kids tuned in regularly to hear Mary Grannan read her "Just Mary" stories, and Saturday night stay-at-homes could turn the dial and dance to the bands of Percy Faith, Luigi Romanelli, Horace Lapp and Mart Kenny, broadcast live from hotel ballrooms.

When the postman came to the door (even on Saturdays), he may have dropped off any of a dozen Canadian magazines: *New Liberty*, *Canadian Home Journal*, *New World*, *Canadian Homes and Gardens*, *Mayfair* or others that had been published for years. Most Canadian periodicals carried short stories, serialized novels and poetry, a welcome source of income for writers.

It was the beginning of the heyday of photo journalism, and the *Star Weekly* and the *Montreal Standard* transcribed the week's news into sensational picture stories. Television, an astounding new technological development that was making headlines in the United States, was a gadget of the future for most Canadians.

nuts and bolts

For the first five years of the forties, Canada had been occupied with the business of war, and for the remainder of the decade with the nuts-and-bolts of building factories and mills, homes and highways, and healthy bank balances. Some things, like the blossoming of opera, ballet, live theatre and painting, and the frills of fancy restaurants serving imported wines, espresso, brioche and brie, Canadians would have to wait for. In the meantime, what was wrong with Canadian cheddar and penny mining stocks? The neighborhood movie houses gave away bone china cups and saucers. And "Uncle Louis" St. Laurent played bridge in his new home at 24 Sussex Drive. Everything was just fine.

Radio was in its golden years when CBC public forum shows like "What's Your Beef? gave listeners the chance to air their gripes in front of a panel of celebrities. Recognize any faces? From the left: Reid Forsee, Greg Clark, Gordon Sinclair, (unidentified), Foster Hewitt and producer Don Sims.

Saturday's Heroes

Through the years of war and peace, professional and amateur athletes gave Canadians something to cheer about. Syl Apps, Teeder Kennedy and Turk Broda led the Leafs to five Stanley Cups. The Calgary Stampeders and their fans transformed the Grey Cup into a national whoop-up. Barbara Ann Scott became the world's figure skating champ and Canada's darling. Ken Watson's rink won three consecutive Briers in curling. In boxing, Jackie Callura held the world featherweight title. Gérard Côté won the Boston Marathon four times. George Woolf was the top jockey, and George Chenier was the snooker king.

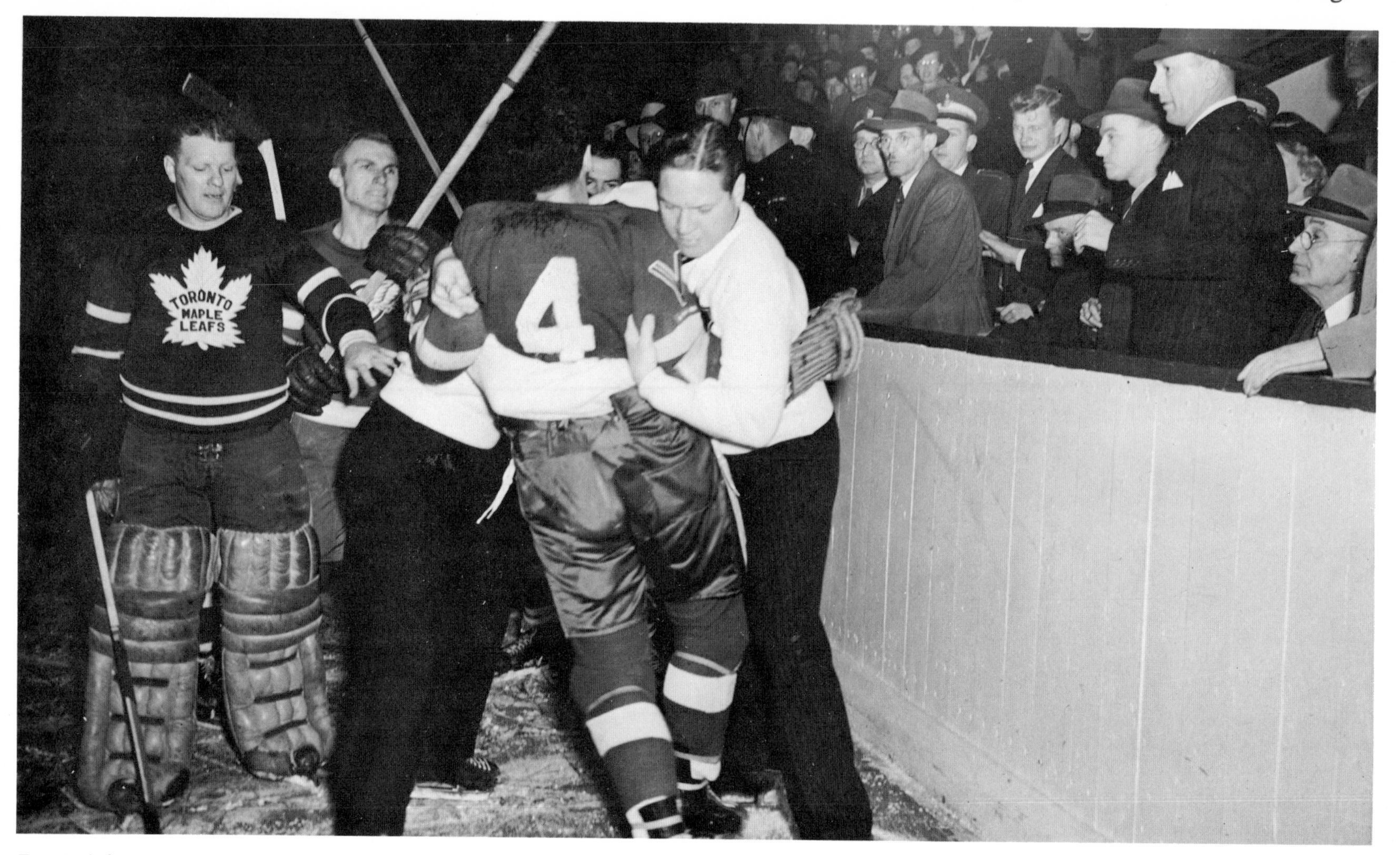

Fans in fedoras catch a blow-by-blow view of this donnybrook between the Detroit Red Wings and the Toronto Maple Leafs, as goalie Turk Broda looks on.

Montreal's Johnny Greco, seen here (left), KO'd this opponent before he got a crack at Rocky Graziano and the world middleweight crown in 1948.

Acknowledgements

Reminiscences of friends, acquaintances and other contemporaries greatly helped in giving substance to memories, emotions and events of the decade. Among those who helped with that part of *A Time of Heroes* were Bill Zeleny, Marion Fosket, Nels Scaravelli, Elaine Campbell, Dick Roberts, Barbara DaPrato, Bob Gaby, Elaine Knight, Charles Gage and Alec Sturton. The assistance of historians and librarians at the National Library, the Public Archives of Canada, the Directorate of History at National Forces headquarters, the Metropolitan Toronto Central Reference Library, and the Royal Canadian Legion is also acknowledged with gratitude.

Stephen Franklin

The Author

Stephen Franklin has worked for many years as a writer in Ottawa, Montreal, Edmonton, Vancouver and Toronto on newspapers and magazines, and in television and films. During the forties he served at sea for six years aboard corvettes and motor torpedo boats before joining the North Bay *Daily Nugget* as a reporter. A long-time student of social history, he earned a Southam Fellowship at the University of Toronto in the sixties. Among his previous books is *Knowledge Park*, a futuristic novel about the establishment of a world information centre.

Index

The page numbers in italics refer to illustrations and captions

Advertising, *7, 12, 13, 52, 60, 69, 78, 79, 85,* 88
Aircraft, *1, 7,* 13, 37, *45*
Avro Anson, 37
Catalina, *38,* 41
Focke-Wulf, 39
Halifax, *39,* 42
Hawker Hurricane, 11, 12, 15
Lancaster, 13, *35, 42,* 42-43, 61, *65*
Lockheed, *8*
Messerschmitt, 39, *44*
Mosquito, 13, 39, 69
Spitfire, 39, 41, 44-45
Wellington, *34*
Aircraft industry, 11, 12, 13, *65*
Air-raid precautions, *74, 76*
Air raids, *32, 39,* 41-44, 57-58, 61
Alberta, 105-7, *106, 111*
Alcan Highway, *16,* 105, *110*
Allen, Ralph, *27,* 58-60, 119
Anglin, Gerald, 113
Anticosti Island, 52, *55*
Apps, Syl, 122
Arcand, Adrien, 70
Army, *6*
Canadian Forestry Corps, 33
Canadian Women's Army Corps, *19,* 33, 61, 63, 64
Essex Scottish Regiment, 84
First Army, 32, 41
Hastings and Prince Edward Regiment, 32
No. 2 Canadian Film and Photo Unit, 60
Ontario Regiment, 32
parachute troops, 32
pay, 8
Régiment de la Chaudière, 31
Royal Canadian Army Medical Corps, 33
Royal Canadian Artillery, *22,* 26
Royal Hamilton Light Infantry, 29
Royal Regiment of Canada, 29
Royal Rifles, 28
Royal 22nd Regiment, 27, 32, *85*
South Saskatchewan Regiment, 29
Third Division, *23,* 26, 33, 60
Winnipeg Grenadiers, 28
Army, British, 26, 27, 32
Army Show, 63, 64
Army vehicles, 14, *31*
Army, German, 25, 28, 32
Arnhem, *33*
Arvida, Que., 15
Asbestos strike, *108,* 108, *109*
Athens, 54
Atlantic, Battle of the, *47,* 49-54, *49, 50,* 55, *55*
Atomic bomb, 101, 103
Atomic Energy Commission, 102
Atomic Energy Control Board, *29*
Audet, Dick, 39
Automobiles, 14, *117*

Bachle, Leo, *90*
Balloon bombs, *67*
Bannock, Russell, 39
Banting, Frederick, *42*
Baum, Gregory, 95
Beaverbrook, Lord, 11
Belgium, 11, 25, 26
Bell, Cyrus Vaughan, *90*
Bell, Ken, 60
Belsen, *94*
Bennett, R. B., 115
Berton, Pierre, 102
Beurling, George F., *43,* 44-45
Birchall, Leonard, 41
Birney, Earle, 7, *26,* 119
Bjerring, Gudrun, 61-62
Blume, Helmut, *93,* 95
Bobak, Molly Lamb, 61
Bouvier, Damase, 64
Bracken, John, *86*
Brandon, Tom, 85
Bremerhaven, 98
Britain, Battle of, 12
British Broadcasting Corporation 57, 81
British Columbia, 76
British Commonwealth and Empire, 9, 26, 115, 118
British Commonwealth Air Training Plan, 37
British Security Co-ordination, *69,* 75, *75*
Broda, Turk, *122*
Brooke, Margaret, 53
Brophy, Pat, 42-43
Burk, Charles, 55
Bushnell, Ernest, 58
Bush pilots, 37, 43

Caen, 32, 60
Cahen, Oscar, 95
Calendars, *110-11*
Callan, Les, *59*
Callura, Jackie, *122*
Cameron, Colin, 7
Cameron, Earl, 57
Camp X, 75
Canada at War, 9, 64
"Canada Carries On," 62, *64*
Canadian Broadcasting Corporation, 57-58, *66,* 75, 103, 120, *121*
"Canadian Cavalcade," *60,* 120
Canadian Confederation of Catholic Workers, 108
Canadian Congress of Labour, 107
Canadian Legion, 88
Canadian Press, 29, 58, 60
Carr, Emily, 95
Carr, Sam, 103
Carson, Kit, 64
Cartoons, *26, 55, 58, 59, 70, 84, 86, 128*
Casualties, *6,* 8-9, 29, *30,* 32, *39,* 53, *53,* 54, 88
Ceylon, 28, 41
Chalk River Nuclear Laboratories, 102
Chambers, Jack, *53, 70*
Charbonneau, Joseph, 108, *109*
Chenier, George, *122*
Chisholm, Brock, 115
Churchill, Winston, 11, *56,* 62, 75, *75,* 115
Cigarettes, *95,* 107
Clark, Gregory, 58, *121*
Cloutier, Albert, *35*
Cobalt 60 Beam Therapy Unit, 102
Cold War, *101*
Coldwell, M. J., *86,* 98
Comfort, Charles, *24, 25,* 61, *62*
Comic books, *90-91*
Communist Party (Labour-Progressive), 70, 103
Concentration camps, *94,* 95
Conscription, 15, 26, 33, *70*
Conservative Party, *86*
Convoys, 49-50, 51, 52, 57
Cook, J. A. M., 58
Co-operative Commonwealth Federation, 7, 9, *72, 86,* 98
Côté, Gérard, *122*
Coughlin, Bing, *59*
Coughlin, Charles, 71
Courseulles-sur-Mer, *23,* 32
Coward, Noel, 64

Dancing, 13, 27, *27*
D-Day, *23, 31,* 32, *46,* 54, 58, 60, *111*
Deep River, Ont., 102
Degaussing device, 15
De la Roche, Mazo, 119
Dempsey, Lotta, *78*
Deutschbund, 70
DeWolf, Harry, 54-55
Dieppe raid, 29, *30*
Dingle, Adrian, *90, 91*
Dionne, J. Ludger, 98
Displaced Persons, 93-94, 97, *98,* 98-99
Dixon, F. L., 84
Dominion-Provincial Conference (1945), *115*
Douglas, T. C., 7-8, 9
Doukhobors, 71
Drapeau, Jean, 108
Drew, George, 97
Drew-Brook, Tom, 75
Dring, William, *36, 37*
Drury, C. M., 99
Duberville, Frank, 60
Dunkirk evacuation, 25, 26
Duplessis, Maurice, *99,* 105, *108,* 108, *109*

Easton, Alan, 50
Eaton, John David, 43
Eldorado Mine, 101
Election, federal (1940), 15
Ellis, Jean, 33, 81
Engbrecht, Peter, 42
Espionage, 69-70, *69,* 75-76, *75,* 95, 103

Fackenheim, Emil, 95
Faith, Percy, 120
Family allowances, 9, *86,* 86, 119
Fascists, Canadian, 69, 70
Fashion, *17,* 18, *78,* 107, 113-14
Fauquier, John, 43
Fiction, 7, *26, 27, 78,* 119-20, *119*
Film, documentary, 60-61, 61-64
Finnish Canadians, 13

Firestone, O. J., 95
Foote, John, 29
Forsee, Reid, *121*
France, fall of, 11, 15, 25, 37
France, liberation of, 26, 58-60
Franks, William R., 15, *42*
Fuchs, Klaus, 95
Fuller, Tom, 55
Funk, Johnny, 107

Garner, Hugh, 119
Gaspé Peninsula, 51-52, 69
Gélinas, Gratien, 119
German Canadians, 13, 71
Gestapo, 69, 76, *93*
Godbout, Adélard, *99*
Goodeve, Charles, 15
Goranson, Paul, *34*
Gordon, Donald, 15
Gould, Glenn, 95
Goulet, Robert, 64
Gouzenko, Igor, *64*, 103, *103*, *104*
Graham, Gwethalyn, 119
Grannan, Mary, 120
Grant, Freddie, 64, *81*
Greber, Jacques, 99
Greco, Johnny, *123*
Greene, Lorne, 57, *60*, 62
Grey Cup, *122*
Grierson, John, 61-62, *64*, *66*
G-Suit, 15, 20, *42*

Halifax, 49, 50, 95, *96*
  VE Day riots, 81-82, *84*
Halton, Matthew, 57
Hanratty, Ted, 87
Happy Gang, *57*
Harris, Lawren Phillips, *2*
Hartwig, Paul, 52-53
Harvison, Clifford, 69
Hewitt, Foster, *121*
Hings, Donald, 15
Hiroshima, 100, 101
Hitler, Adolf, 7, 25, 29, 81
Hitschmanova, Lotta, 99
Holland, 99
  conquest of, 11, 25
  liberation of, 26, 33, *33*
Holmes, Art, 57-58
Homburger, Walter, 95
Hong Kong, surrender of, 28, 83
Houde, Camillien, 70-71, *71*
Houle, Len, 64
Housing, 87, *107*
Howe, C. D., 15, *15*, 95
Hungarian Canadians, 13
Hunter, Vern, 105
Hutchison, Bruce, 75
Hutterites, 71

Ilsley, J. L., 15
Immigrants and immigration, 9, 93-94, 97-99, *97*
Indian Ocean, *38*, 41
Internees, 64, 70-71, *72*, *73*, *81*, *93*, 94-95
Irving, K. C., 13
Italian campaign, *2*, *22*, *24*, *31*, 32, 57, 61
Italian Canadians, 12, 70

Jamieson, Don, 118
Janowski, Werner, 69
Japanese Canadians, *72*, *73*, 76-77
Jehovah's Witnesses, 71
Jive, *120*
Johnny Canuck, *90*
Juliana of the Netherlands, 99

Kander, Gerhard, *93*
Kennedy, Teeder, *122*
Kenny, Mart, 120
King, William Lyon Mackenzie, 15, 26, 33, 37, *56*, *70*, 82, *86*, *93*, *99*, *104*, 113, 114-15, *115*, *118*
King George VI, 9, 115
Krivitsky, Alexei, *103*
Krupp factories, 41-42
Ku Klux Klan, 70
Kuper, Jack, 99

Labine, Gilbert, 101
LaMarsh, Judy, 86
Larsen, Henry, 119
Laurence, George C., 101
Law, Tony, 55
Leacock, Stephen, 9
Leduc, Alta., 105-7, *106*, *111*
Lehmann, Karl, 76
Lévesque, Georges-Henri, *108*
Liberal Party, 9, 15, *72*, 114-15, *118*, 118
Liquor laws, 88
Luftwaffe, 11, 41, *44*, 45, 57
Lumsden, A. L., *38*
Lund, Alan and Blanche, 64

Macalister, John, 76
McDougall, John, 61
Macfarlane, R. A., 105
MacGill, Elsie Gregory, 12
MacGillivray, Kenneth, 105
McKay, R. W., 15
Mackenzie, C. J., 101
McKnight, Elmer, *81*
McLaren, Norman, 62
MacLennan, Hugh, *119*, 120
McNaughton, A. G. L., *29*
Magazines, 61, *66*, *78-79*
  Canadian Home Journal, 120
  Chatelaine, *78*
  Maclean's, 26, *55*, 71, *79*, 102
  Montreal Standard, 58, 120
  National Home Monthly, *78*
  New Liberty, 120
  New World, *113*, 120
  Relations, 108
  Revue Populaire, *79*
  Star Weekly, 58, 120
Malta, *43*, 44
Manning, E. C., 107
Marchand, Jean, *108*, 108
Maritime Provinces, 51-52
Marriage, 86-87, *107*
Massey Commission, *108*
May, Alan Nunn, 103
"Meet the Navy", *63*, 64
Mennonites, 71
Merritt, Cecil, 29
Meyer, Kurt, 32
Milne, Gilbert, 60
Miss Canada Contest, *114*
Montgomery, Bernard, 32
Moore, K. O., 41
Morris, Jerrold, *34*
Munro, Ross, 29, 58
Murmansk route, 54
Murray, Gladstone, 75
Music, *93*, 95, *120*, 120
Mynarski, Andy, 42-43

Nadeau, Rita, 64
Nagasaki, 101
National Film Board, 61-64, *64*, *66*, 103
National registration, 15, 70, *71*
National Research Council, 101, 103
National Resources Mobilization Act, 15, 26
Nelson, Joyce, 11
Newfoundland, 115-19, *118*
Newspapers, 57, 61
  Calgary *Albertan*, *83*
  Fort William *Times*, 13
  Leduc *Representative*, 107
  Maple Leaf, *59*, *82*
  Montreal *Devoir*, *71*, 108
  Montreal *Presse*, *71*
  Montreal *Star*, 37
  Ottawa *Journal*, 103, *104*
  Port Arthur *Chronicle*, 13
  Toronto Daily Star, *104*
  Toronto *Evening Telegram*, 81, *83*
  Toronto *Globe and Mail*, 58-60
  Vancouver News-Herald, *83*
  Vancouver *Province*, 7
  Vancouver *Sun*, 75
  Winnipeg *Free Press*, 58, 61-62
  Winnipeg *Tribune*, 81
Nichols, Jack, 61
Nissen hut, *40*, *41*
Normandy campaign, *31*, 32, 60-61
North African campaign, 14, 27, 28
North Vancouver, B.C., 14, *74*
Northwest Passage, 119
Nuclear energy, 101-2

Odell, G. K., *66*
Oil, 105-7, *106*, *111*
Olympic Games (1948), *112*, 113
Ortona, *22*, *31*, 32
Ottawa, 15, *80*, 87, 99
Ouimet, Marcel, 57

Pacific War, 15, 28, *38*, 83
Paris, 58-60
Patterson, Fuller, 37
Patterson, George, 103
Pavlov, Antoni, 103
Peace River country, 105
Pearl Harbor, 12, 28, *72*, *76*, 76
Pearson, Drew, 103
Pearson, L. B., 99, 115
Peenemünde, 43-44
Pelletier, Gérard, 108
Pickersgill, Frank, 76
Pin-ups, 27, *28*
Pitt, Arnold, 15
Polish Canadians, 13, 42
Port Hope, Ont. 101

Posters, *4, 11, 64, 66, 67, 68, 77*
Power, C. G., 39
Pratt, E. J., 119
Pratt, John, *63,* 64
Price controls, 18, *21, 85*
Prices, 52, 84, *85,* 107
Prisoner-of-war camps, *63,* 76, *81,*
85, *94, 95*
Proximity fuse, 15
Purcell, Gillis, 60

Quakers, 71
Quebec Conference, *56*
Quebec Provincial Police, 108, *109*

Racial and religious bigotry, 71,
72, 73, 76-77, 93, *99*
Radar, 15, 29
Radio, 57-58, *57, 60, 116,* 118, 120, *121*
Railways, 7, 13, 105
Ralston, J. L., *29,* 33
Rationing and shortages, *12, 18,*
18-20, *21*
Recruiting, *4,* 8
Red Cross, 33, 95
Reeve, Ted, *59*
Refrigeration, *88,* 88
Roads, 7, 105
Roberts, Leslie, *101*
"Rodeo Rhythm," 64
Romanelli, Luigi, 120
Rommel, Erwin, 14, 28
Roosevelt, Franklin D., 37, *56,* 75,
75, 115
Rose, Fred, 103
Roy, Gabrielle, 119
Royal Air Force, 11, 37-38, *43,* 41-45
Royal Canadian Air Force, 9, *19, 34,*
35, 36, 37-45, *37, 40, 41, 42, 43,*
45, 83
Coastal Command, 39-41
Digby Wing, 41
No. 401 Squadron, *44*
No. 413 Squadron, *38,* 41
No. 6 Bomber Group, 41-43
Pathfinder Squadron, 43
Women's Division, 38-39, *63*
Royal Canadian Mounted Police, 69,
70, 76, 103, *103,* 119
Royal Canadian Navy, 11-12, *47, 48,*
49-55, *50, 51, 52, 53, 54*
Women's Royal Canadian Naval
Service, 55, *63,* 64
Royal Navy, 8, 15
Russell, Harold, 88

Sabotage, 77
Sabourin, Roméo, 76
St. Laurent, Louis S., 103, 115, 119, 120
St. Lawrence, Battle of the, 52-54, *55*
Salvage campaigns, 41
Scandinavian Canadians, 13
Scheldt Estuary, 32
Schull, Joseph, 51
Scott, Barbara Ann, *112,* 113
Secrecy, *49, 52,* 52, *68, 77*
Shapiro, Lionel, 58
Sherbrooke, Que., *94,* 94, 95
Shipbuilding, 11-12, 13-14
Ships and boats
aircraft carriers, 41
battleships, 41, 50
corvettes, 11-12, 14, *48,* 49,
50-51, 52, 53, *53*
cruisers, 41, 50, 82
destroyers, 14, 41, *47,* 49, 50, 54-55
E-boats, 55
ferries, 53
freighters, 13, 49, 51, 52, 53
frigates, 14, 51, *53*
grain carriers, 13
I-boats, 55
landing craft, 54
liners, 25, 49
minesweepers, 13, 50
MTBs, 55
schooners, 55, 119
submarines, 14, *34,* 41, *47,* 49-50,
49, 51-53, *51, 74,* 76
tankers, 13, 49, *51*
troop transports, 53, *82,* 82
Shuster, Frank, *63,* 64
Sicily, invasion of, 26, 32, 58
Silver Cross mothers, 9
Sims, Don, *121*
Sinclair, Gordon, *121*
Slotin, Louis, *101, 102*
Smallwood, Joseph R., *118,* 119
Songs, *25, 37,* 64, *81*
Sports, *122, 123*
SS (Schutzstaffel), 32, 76, *94*
Stacey, C. P., 71
Stanley Cup, *122*
Station M, 75
Stephenson, William, 62, 69, 75,
75, 103
Sterling, Geoff, 118
Stern, Max, 95
Stratford, Ont., *117*
Strikes, 107-8
Sudbury, Ont., 14, 83

Tanks, *2,* 15, *33*
Taxes, 9, 14, 18
Telephone, *20*
Tito, Josip Broz, 28-29, 75
Trades and Labour Congress, 107
Trade unions, 9, 13, 107
Trans-Canada Airlines, 7, *8,* 13
Trans-Canada Highway Act, 105
Triquet, Paul, 32
Trudeau, Pierre Elliott, 108
Turta, Mike, 105, 107

Udet, Ernst, *43,* 44
Ukrainian Canadians, 12
Unemployment, 12
Unemployment insurance, 9, *87,* 118
Union Nationale, *99,* 105
Unitarian Service Committee, 99
United Auto Workers, 13
United Jewish Relief, 99
United Nations, *29,* 102, 115
United States entry into war, 51-52
Universities, 85-86
British Columbia, 77, 85
Laval, *108*
McGill, 95, 101
Toronto, 15, *42,* 85-86, 95
Uranium, 101, 103
Utas, Gus, *43*

Vancouver, *6,* 38, *76, 83,* 87
Vancouver Island, *74,* 76
VE Day, *80,* 81-2, *82, 84*
Venereal disease, *67*
Veterans' Guard, 76
Veterans' return and rehabilitation,
83-86, *84, 85, 89, 107*
Victoria Cross, 29, 32, 43
Victory Bonds, *4, 11, 13,* 20, *64,* 66
VJ Day, 82-83, *83*
Volunteer work, 20
V-1 rockets, 39, 43

Wage controls, 18, *21*
Wages, 13, 84, 98, 99, 107, 108
Walkie-talkie, 15, 20
War artists, *2, 23, 24, 34, 35, 36, 37,*
48, 53, 54, 61, *62*
War brides 27, 38, 86, *92, 93,* 95,
96, 116
War correspondents, 29, 57-60
War industries, *4, 10,* 11-15, *11, 12,*
15, 16-17, 20, *65*
War Savings Certificates, 13, 62
Wartime Information Board, *9,* 62,
64, 66
Wartime Prices and Trade Board, 15, 18
Watson, Ken, *122*
Wayne, Johnny, *63,* 64
Welfare legislation, 9, *86,* 118-19
Werra, Franz von, 76
West Indies, 52
Wheat, 8, 13, 14, *110*
Whitton, Charlotte, 95
Wilkie, Agnes, 53
Wilson, Cairine, 94
Wilson, Ethel, 120
Women
in forces, *19,* 33, 38-39, 55, 61,
63, *63,* 64
in industry, *10,* 11-12, *14, 16-17, 65*
Women's Christian Temperance Union,
88
Wood, Tom, *23, 48*
Woodsworth, J. S., 7
Woolf, George, *122*

Young Women's Christian Association,
95
Yugoslavia, 28-29
Yukon Territory, 105

Zabotin, Nicolai, 103
Zaroubin, Gyorgi, *104*
Zinn, Walter, 101
"Zombies," 26, 32, 33

Picture Credits

--Drawn for Maclean's by Ben Roth.

"I'll bet peace catches me right in the middle of a big pull-over with sleeves!"

We would like to acknowledge the help and co-operation of the directors and staff of the various public institutions and the private firms and individuals who made available paintings, posters, mementoes, collections and albums as well as photographs, and gave us permission to reproduce them. Every effort has been made to identify and credit appropriately the sources of all illustrations used in this book. Any further information will be appreciated and acknowledged in subsequent editions.

The illustrations are listed in the order of their appearance on the page, left to right, top to bottom. Principal sources are credited under these abbreviations:

PAC	Public Archives of Canada
MTL	Metropolitan Toronto Library
PC	Private Collection
SN	*Saturday Night*
CP	Canadian Press
M	*Maclean's* Magazine
CW	Canada Wide, Montreal Star
CWM	Canada War Museum, National Museum of Man, National Museums of Canada

/1 Hignell Printing Limited /2 CWM 12722 /4 MTL /6 Claude Dettloff /7 PC /8 Air Canada /9 PAC /10 Miller Services /11 PAC /12 PC /13 SN /14 Toronto Transit Commission 14631 /15 Fednews /16 PAC 119767; Canada Cycle and Motor /17 Toronto *Sun* /18 PAC (Montreal *Gazette*) PA108300 /19 CP /20 PC /21 PC /22 National Gallery of Canada /23 National Gallery of Canada /24 CWM 12296 /25 PC /26 PC /27 PAC (DND) 48935; PAC (DND) 52722 /28 PAC (DND) 31434 /29 PAC (L.A. Audrian) /30 PAC Z8471-11 /31 PAC (DND) 27443; CP; CP; PAC (DND) 36285 /32 Wide World Photos /33 PAC (DND) 50084 /34 CWM 11356 /35 CWM 10905 /36 CWM 7809 /37 The National Library of Canada /38 PAC PL10095 /39 PAC (DND) 32846 /40 PAC PL40964 /41 PAC 33441 /42 Institute of Aviation Medicine, Toronto; CP /43 Royal Canadian Air Force; PAC PL28520 /44 PAC PL22146 /45 CWM 2-3-12 /46 CWM 12468 /47 CWM 10033 /48 CWM 10572 /49 PAC C33443 /50 PAC (DND) NP904-A /51 PAC TC930 /52 SN; 52-53 PAC (DND) GM1441 /53 PAC C44317 /54 CWM 10503 /55 M /56 National Film Board /57 SN /58 PAC (DND) 24261 /59 *The Maple Leaf* /60 PC; PAC (DND) 2403 /61 PC; PAC (DND) 19902 /62 CP /63 PAC (DND) 2-2374-56; Canadian Armed Forces; PC /64 PAC /65 M /66 PC /67 Imperial War Museum /68 MTL /69 Toronto *Sun* /70 PAC C24354 /71 PAC PA47186 /72 PAC C47387; PAC C26386 /73 PAC C46350 /74 Vancouver Public Library /75 Harcourt Brace Jovanovich /76 PC /77 MTL /78 PC /79 PC /80 PAC /81 PC /82 PAC (DND) 56405 /83 Toronto *Sun;* The Calgary *Albertan;* The *Vancouver News-Herald* /84 M; PAC (DND) /85 PC; Archives Nationales du Québec /86 PAC C44323; Winnipeg *Free Press* /87 PC /88 PC /89 Foote Collection, Manitoba Archives /90 PC /91 PC /92 CP /93 SN /94 CP; PAC (DND) Z-2907-3 /95 SN /96 CW /97 CW /98 Wide World Photos /99 SN /100 Wide World Photos /101 PC /102 Wide World Photos /103 CP /104 MTL /105 PAC PA47655 /106 PC /107 PAC NL5390 /108 PAC C16986 /109 PAC C53641 /110 PC /111 PC /112 Newton Photographic Associates /113 PC 114 Herb Nott & Co. /115 M /116 CW /117 M /118 PAC /119 Nakash, Montreal /120 PC /121 Canada Pictures (Toronto) /122 Alexandra Studio /123 CW /128 M

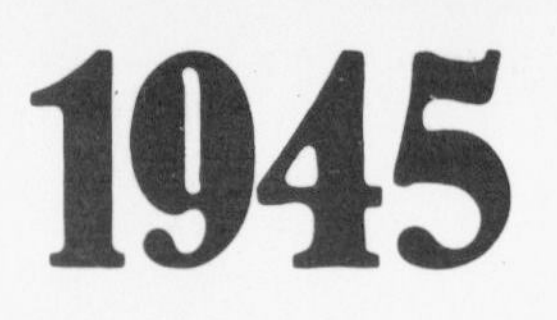

1945

Canada signs United Nations charter at San Francisco.

Germany surrenders on May 8 (VE Day), ending war in Europe.

The Albertan

OFFICIAL V-E DAY TUESDAY, MAY 8

'Now We Can Really Get Started' Say Pacific Troops

FOE FIGHT ON IN CZECHOSLOVAKIA

Surrender Is Signed But Leaders Hold Up Final Announcements

Growth and Decline of Hitler Germany

Tokyo Next Target

General Refuses To Stop Fighting

VE Day riots in Halifax cause estimated $5 million in damages.

General election returns Liberals to power with narrow majority.

First "Baby Bonus" cheques issued under Family Allowance Bill.

U.S. drops atomic bombs on Hiroshima and Nagasaki, Japan.

THE VANCOUVER DAILY PROVINCE

ATOMIC BOMB DROPPED ON JAPAN

Ottawa Plans $30 Pension Monthly For All Over 70

"A FRONTLINE GENERAL"

Equals 20,000 Tons Explosive

What Ottawa's "New Deal" Proposes

10,000 Sockeye Stranded

B.C. May Lose Financially By 'New Deal'

Today in Europe

Dominion-Provincial Conference on Reconstruction meets in Ottawa.

Japan surrenders on August 15 (VJ Day), ending war in Pacific.

Igor Gouzenko defects from Soviet Embassy with details of spy ring.

Average annual income: $1,538.

Hugh MacLennan publishes *Two Solitudes*.

Canada's first nuclear reactor begins operation at Chalk River, Ont.

Department of Veterans' Affairs established to co-ordinate repatriation programme.

Gabrielle Roy publishes *Bonheur d'occasion (The Tin Flute)*.

1946

Saskatchewan introduces first programme of socialized medicine.

Veterans seize Victoria Hall to protest Vancouver's housing shortage.

Royal Commission on espionage activities links 12 Canadians with Soviet spy ring.

TORONTO DAILY STAR

40 TO 50 HELD IN SPY CASE

RUSSIA NAMED BY MINISTER

FEDERAL CIVIL SERVANTS RESEARCH MEN ACCUSED

HOME AND SPORT EDITION

SPY HUNT MAY SPREAD TO WASHINGTON—REPORT

Harold Russell of Nova Scotia wins Academy Award for *The Best Years of Our Lives*.

Atomic Energy Commission of Canada established.

CNE grandstand destroyed by fire.

Schooner *Bluenose* sinks after hitting reef off Haiti.

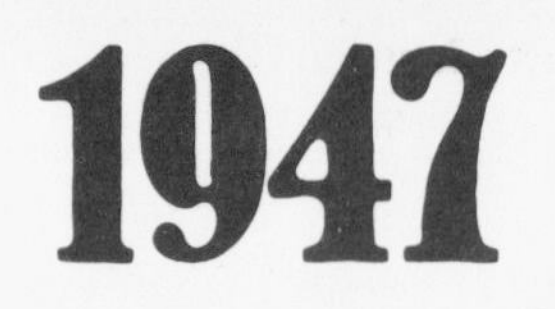

1947

Snag, Y.T. registers –81°F., lowest temperature recorded in North America.

Oil discoveries at Leduc, Alta. start drilling boom.

Canada elected member of the U.N. Security Council.

Food rationing ends.

Post-war immigration of displaced persons from Europe begins.

Question

How wide should Canada's doors be opened after the war?

What restrictions would you want to see imposed?

Apart from the British, what races would you welcome?